Track Conditions

Also by Michael Klein

POETRY
1990

Day and Paper (1998)

ANTHOLOGIES
Poets for Life: Seventy-Six Poets Respond to AIDS

Things Shaped in Passing:
More "Poets for Life" Writing from the AIDS Pandemic
(with Richard McCann)

In the Company of My Solitude:
American Writing from the AIDS Pandemic
(with Marie Howe)

Track Conditions

a memoir

Michael Klein

PERSEA BOOKS   NEW YORK

So that a time, more than its people, be honored
as truthfully as my recollection allows,
many of the names in this book have been changed.—M.K.

For information, write to the publisher:

Persea Books, Inc.
171 Madison Avenue
New York, New York 10016

Library of Congress Cataloging-in-Publication Data

Klein, Michael, 1954 Aug. 1—
Track conditions : a memoir / Michael Klein.
p.   cm.
ISBN 0-89255-225-5 (hardcover : alk. paper)
1. Klein, Michael, 1954 Aug. 17-   —Biography.   2. Poets,
American—20th century—Biography.   3. Racetracks (Horse racing)-
-United States.   4. Gay men—United States—Biography.   5. Race
horses—Grooming.   I. Title.
PS3561.L349Z47   1997
811'.54—dc21
[B]   96-37647
                                                            CIP

Articles and excerpts from articles published in The New York Times,
copyright © 1984 by The New York Times Co. Reprinted by permission.

Designed by REM Studio, Inc.
Typeset in Adobe Garamond by Keystrokes, Lenox, Massachusetts.
Printed and bound by The Haddon Craftsmen, Scranton, Pennsylvania.

FIRST EDITION

Contents

v

Contents

Contents

For Richard Coatney,
who gave me horses

Let us lay aside every weight, and the sin which doth so easily beset us,
and let us run with patience the race that is set before us.

HEBREWS 12:1

Track Conditions

One

———————

Runaway Groom

I ran away. I was fifteen. I ran away for a break from what my stepfather was doing, from New York, from being a twin and drinking too much through a musical education. I ran away for some harmony and some sex.

And I landed at a drop-in center in New Haven, the town I'd lived in with my natural father after the divorce. The drop-in center had a piano in the hallway and a stranger at a card table. The light buzzed like an old refrigerator. When I sat down to play the piano, the stranger came over and sat beside me.

"I like the way you sing," the stranger said.

"What do you like about it?"

"You try to hit notes you can't always reach."

"That's good?"

"Yeah. It's brave."

His name was Carl and he was tall and thin with luminous, long black hair. He took me to his house, which was down some streets I'd remembered from years before. Yale's streets: streets of lighted globes on apartment buildings, streets of trees.

I stayed with Carl for a week and tried to locate the part of myself that could be intimate with a man I didn't know—which meant that I drank. I started drinking when I was twelve, to make passion easier. When I was drunk, I could fall into a stranger's sheets—desire without fear.

Running away solved nothing, but that peculiar rhythm of departure became a theme. Almost ten years later, I ran away again, in a chase after my lover Richard Coatney, who ran away from me and from New York because of my drinking problem. My adult self, more practiced than the teenager experimenting in New Haven, had rationalized that I was drinking in grief over my mother who'd died in 1977 (suicide or heart attack, no one knew for sure).

Richard had left me for River Downs, a racetrack in Cincinnati. His father was a trainer there, so in a way he'd returned home. The racetrack may have been in another world, a wrong turn for me off an already unsteady road, but

I was in love with someone who'd actually lived there. Once I got to the track myself, I could see immediately that this was a world that suited Richard. A week out of New York and he was already a different person—sunnier. He'd even stopped smoking—an extremely radical move, it seemed to me.

How strange racehorses were to me then. As strange, I suppose, as when I first saw them charging down the stretch one spring afternoon before I was a runaway. My family had just moved to Brooklyn, and my stepfather was driving me into the sun. The mysteries of life as they were happening were often revealed in the Vista Cruiser. Today's mystery was why we had left a glorious apartment on Central Park West to live in a nondescript two-family house in Coney Island. A leap, to be sure.

"Because we can't afford to live like that anymore."

"Why not?"

"Because I lost a lot of money on horses."

I'd learned by watching my stepfather's addiction to gambling for the past five years how it soured his marriage to my mother and locked his inquisitive mind into a dull job. I had also figured out that winning or losing had nothing to do with gambling. The thrill between desire and the shadow of desire confused time and currency for the compulsive. Gambling was like spending money in a dream.

On Monday nights, we had gone as a family to Gamblers Anonymous in the fluorescently lit basement of a church off Ocean Parkway. I didn't understand what was going on exactly, but I could quickly see that any real interest in the meetings merely flashed in and out of my stepfather's eyes like lighted numbers on a carnival wheel. He had a short attention span when it came to the outside world telling him the story of his life and had no intention of letting G.A. help him stop gambling. I suppose my stepfather hadn't lost enough—that is, hadn't lost everything.

We were driving down Coney Island Avenue on our way to a baseball game. I hated baseball, but I was having sex with my stepfather and it was hard to find another way to be alone together. We had sex in the car most of the time—mechanically, in sitting positions. The sexual relationship had started when I was twelve or thirteen. I initiated it because my stepfather had been physically abusive to me for years—hitting me with a chair, punching me, wrestling me down to the ground. Sex seemed to me, even at that age, the way to diminish his force—of meeting him without being overtaken by him. If I could usher him erotically forward, he wouldn't cancel me.

Of course, I had relationships with my mother and twin brother, Kevin, but these seemed meaningful only as hiding places from my stepfather. He had us all terrified, which made him as darkly intoxicating as a cyclone that could destroy any one of us. My sex with him meant not being destroyed, but it also kept me confused. I didn't survive the abuse of incest as much as hold it like a candle in front of me to see in the dark.

There was always a sexual undercurrent in the relationship, and my stepfather made remarks to me on a daily basis. Things like "nice ass" and "pretty hair, pretty boy." I never followed through any of the innuendoes until one night when, after a skirmish in the kitchen, he made contact by brushing up against me in his underwear. I reached my hand into the front of his boxer shorts in the blurry gesture of a swoon.

My stepfather was taking me to a baseball game so he could say this to me: "If you tell me the truth, I'll tell you the truth."

"Okay."

"Do you smoke marijuana?"

"Yes."

"Okay. Here's my truth: We're not going to a baseball game."

But we weren't slipping into the erogenous zone, either. We were on our way to Belmont Park, the king of all racetracks, where, more than a decade later, a life I'd been living would stop.

Two

New Rules

Richard once referred to the summer of 1979 as the summer of soft-cock rock, and he was probably talking about the two of us as much as he was dubbing a musical trend. Chris Cross's "Sailing" came on the radio in the green and dusty barn at River Downs with the reliability of a beer ad. The barn was old and in need of paint, but I imagined I'd walked into a cathedral and the music streaming out of the old radio hanging from a nail on the wall wasn't soft-cock rock at all but a hymn.

"I miss your singing," Richard said dreamily, dressed in the green flannel shirt I had given him for Christmas. We were in the middle of the shedrow and he was about to show me which side of the horse to stand on.

"What do you miss about my singing?"

"Its humility," Richard said.

"Hmm. I never think of myself as particularly humble."

"Well, you're not. But you are when you sing."

"I'm humble when I'm drunk, too."

"No. You're loud and obnoxious when you're drunk."

Richard handed me a horse named Over Pond.

"You stand on the horse's left side and lead him with your right hand. And keep him close to you."

"How do I keep the horse from stepping on me?"

"He knows you're there. He's not going to step on you unless you stop paying attention."

If I could do this one thing exactly right (sober, without letting the horse step on me or get away), maybe the relationship with Richard had another chance. Of course, there was a little more to it than that—miles to go before a lasting reconciliation—but it seemed that Richard's anger that had begun so determinedly in New York was a memory now; or perhaps my decision to come after him was turning his anger back the other way—to love.

"Are you glad I'm here?" I said.

"Yeah, sure I'm glad you're here, you crazy fuck. But it's different now. It has to be different. We have to make new rules."

"What new rules?"

"Don't worry, we'll talk about them."

"Rules about drinking?"

"Rules about drinking and rules about not drinking. I love you, but I came here because I wasn't going to stand by while you drank yourself to death."

Richard was tall and thin with red hair and a goatee. He resembled Vincent Van Gogh, and looking at him just then, I was trying hard to remember if I'd been drinking that day we'd first met on a New York street in 1972. I think I was sober, on my way to a drunk.

"I'll try to stop drinking," I said softly.

But trying would never last long. Drinking was my role in the relationship and I put it between us, from the beginning, with the authority of a welder lowering a face shield. I needed to drink, but I also needed Richard, which is why I left New York to begin with. The city I'd once loved had turned on me in blacked-out escapades and endless nights with strangers—all in the shadow of my mother's death. And I was broke. Any friends I could have asked for a loan had vanished. Or I already owed them. I couldn't hold down a job. I could barely hold down a drink—or a cock, for that matter—and would, more often than not, retch all over the body of the poor guy I'd caught in a midnight, moonlit pass long enough to get him into bed. I was also dragging home thugs and heroin addicts—a peculiar band of narcissists. I was every narcissist's dream: a recruiter of narcissists. All they ever gave me was the opportunity to adore them.

Alcohol had also started making me chronically forgetful and I often wouldn't eat, or couldn't because I had no money.

I lived on a seemingly bottomless box of white rice and tap water. All my money went towards rent, and it was never enough—an ongoing juggling act that eventually pulled me straight into landlord court.

On one of my last mornings in the city, I went to a hearing, money balled up in my sweaty palm. I'd been dancing all night at the Anvil—that venerable after-hours club at the edge of New York's meat-packing district. I wasn't appropriately dressed for anything legal at 9:00 A.M.: harem pants left to me in a stage manager's will, a billowy concoction of baby-blue satin that broke away with a Velcro rip at the ankles and crotch. The landlord wouldn't accept a partial payment and threatened to start eviction proceedings, but I left New York before anything legal became necessary—abandoning the apartment and everything in it.

Now I owned nothing and was sleeping among Richard's flannel shirts and books, drawing paper and empty beer bottles. We lived together inside a room of gray cinder block that had no view and slept on foldaway cots that we put together to have sex on—a falling-through-the-crack kind of sex, which made us argue because we were living on top of each other and it made the sex very raw.

The erotic life for Richard and me had often been intermittent. At River Downs, love usually took us only as far up the road as Bill's Bar—a dive that was always advertising a mechanical bull nobody rode. The bar glowed from the jukebox in the corner and all the light suffused into a kind of amber smoke: safety and timelessness. This was why I wanted to drink in bars and not alone in my room. I used to think it was to be in the company of strangers, but it was to be bathed in that peculiar, infinite light.

Richard and I drank together, and although the future would prove that he was an alcoholic too, neither of us knew it then. We were paying attention to my drinking because it was dramatic and unpredictable—the disabler that gave Richard most of the control over the relationship.

As I walked Over Pond, it occurred to me for a minute that I didn't have to drink. Here was a new and seemingly enchanted place where the rules were going to be different and where I wasn't in trouble. I'd always blamed drinking on something: my mother, my failed musical career, the bad neighborhood—but I couldn't blame the racetrack. Not yet, anyway.

I put Over Pond into his stall, which had been luxuriously bedded with fresh straw.

"You know, Richard, we don't know anyone here except each other. It's going to make us or break us."

"Well, it can't get much worse. This is a chance to start again, if you want to."

"I'm here because I want to."

"Are you all right with it?"

"With what?"

"Walking horses every day. You'll be able to groom eventually, but for now it's going to be pretty boring work around here."

"Yeah, I'm all right with it, as long as I'm all right with you."

"Well, you've got to be all right with Buddy and Jewel, too."

Buddy and Jewel Fisk were my bosses and must have wondered what I was doing there, a stranger to the sport of kings. They could clearly see that Richard and I were lovers, I suppose, but they weren't interested in us as a couple. Why should they have been? We were hired hands—transient and negotiable. The fact that we were using racetrack work to wriggle our way out of our own despair wasn't a concern to them.

Buddy and Jewel looked like John Wayne and Ava Gardner and were enigmatic even by racetrack standards. The only thing we knew about them was that they had a daughter, that Buddy was born in Kentucky, and that they had a runner every once in a while. They weren't personal people, though, and what I knew about them was only what I could surmise by looking at them.

One morning, Jewel was gazing into the middle distance after the last set of horses had gone out to the track, a distance lined with momentary hazards: a groom having trouble getting the tack off a horse; a filly not standing still for the blacksmith; sparrows in distress swimming in a necklace of high notes up to the haylofts. Jewel looked resigned but dignified— a survivor of too many natural disasters. She was pale and anxious and regretful—so her voice said—as though the horses would never be enough to fill her and she knew it. I imagined that with Buddy in her life she was too far inside the coupling to do anything for herself alone. Instead, Jewel helped out around the barn and ducked into the stalls, same as her hired hands.

Jewel was kind to us but kinder to horses, and she related to them in a way I grew to admire. There was a tenderness in her voice when she told a horse, "There, now." The *now* in the phrase was heightened like in gospel, when God seems to enter the witness and the vibrant change in register means the singer is making room to accommodate Him.

When it came to the hired hands or getting into the stalls, Buddy stayed away. He had little to say to the grooms and hot-walkers working under his shedrow and left everything—except taking the horses and exercise riders out to the track—to Jewel. I'd also learned in subsequent weeks that Buddy conditioned horses systematically, as if they had the same amount of talent or lack of it. The runners were overtrained and broke down in the exact order of the overtraining, which put the outfit in the constant position of having to ship in new racing stock. And there was an endless supply of it—a wishing well somewhere that kept overflowing with new victims.

Because it was my first racetrack (and I certainly thought at the time that it would be my last one), the simplicity of River Downs struck me profoundly. Everything revealed repeated itself. The barns were laid out in perfectly straight lines separated by little dirt roads (horse paths) like barracks at a boot camp. At the end of the morning, in barn after barn, you could see all the horses poking their heads out, nibbling at the fresh racks of hay a groom had slip-knotted through the screweye over the stall door. Inside each barn, a clay or dirt path that wound around inside the perimeter was used as the walking ring for the horses when they came back hot—and, at times, delirious—from the track.

The landscape was not glamorous, or even very much like the country. There was barely any vegetation, and the overwhelming heat made everything flat and colorless. Any glam-or at River Downs was to be found in the racing aspect of the business, when the public streamed into the grandstand that was shining over the tops of barns, meeting the horizon just after the three-quarter pole. Above the horizon was the club-house, where people could reserve seats and sit at tables and not have to wait in long betting lines. These were the serious horse players—those who could afford to lose money. My stepfather wouldn't have been among them. I imagined him at the races alone, with just enough money for the parking lot: creature among creatures, fingering his short black wavy hair and pushing his gray eyeglasses up off his nose to read the *Daily Racing Form.*

Besides the barns and the clubhouse and grandstand, there were other shelters from storms maybe, but nowhere to hide from what everyone kept warning me were the ravages of rac-ing life: boredom and exhaustion. A two-story cinder block dormitory housed grooms and hotwalkers, and there was a track kitchen, which also served as a kind of community cen-ter. Everyone hung out there getting drunk and playing cards when they weren't working in the stalls or losing money at the races.

The population at River Downs consisted mostly of gam-blers, illegal aliens, and drifty teenagers at the races for the first time. And very few homosexuals. I met Juan one morning in the kitchen after being on the track a week. Juan was a Mexican who worked for a different trainer every week—not unusual for a groom. Most of the help on the track were either hope-lessly drunk or fired for mistreating horses or both. I didn't know what particular dread it was that Juan kept facing or turned him in circles from week to week. All I knew about him was that he looked crazy and vulnerable. I told Juan I was new to the races and asked if he had any advice for me. His eyes were bright with tips.

"Well, you know, they only have three-point-two-percent beer here. You got to get off the track if you want to get drunk," Juan said, as if he had just given me the most important information there was about life on the track. At that point, it probably was, but he couldn't have known why. Juan asked whom I worked for, and when I told him Buddy and Jewel Fisk, he said that Buddy got his hands on a runner every once in a while but that I might have to wait a long time before I'd see one or, better yet, groom one. I wasn't grooming yet, I told him, but was planning to soon.

Then Juan spoke in a tone of voice someone uses to tell you a house is haunted: "I'll give you a tip, if that's what you want. Get a good horse to rub—that's the trick, and it's how anybody's ever going to know you or care about you here—take care of you. You're only as good as the horse you're sitting under."

"Okay, but how good can it get around here? These aren't the greatest horses in the world."

"Well, sure, you're not at Churchill Downs."

"Churchill Downs?"

"These ain't exactly Kentucky Derby horses."

Although I didn't know it then, a time would come when the world would be nothing but Derby horses. On May 1, 1984, Steve Crist, the racing reporter from the *New York*

Times, would be sitting across from me in the track kitchen at Churchill Downs, asking the first question of an interview: "So did you ever dream you'd be grooming a Derby horse?"

Three

The Labyrinth of Luck

Racetrack society vibrates somewhere between the visible and the invisible. There are people you see all the time: the barn help, the trainers, the exercise crew, the men and women who deliver hay and straw and feed. And there are those you see only rarely, if at all: the jockeys, the parimutuel clerks, the owners, the starting-gate crew. Two worlds: the training world and the racing world. I had contact with the racing world only on those occasions when I would lead a horse over to the paddock and wait until the jockey climbed aboard. Jockeys rarely spoke to grooms. And the owners never did—it just wasn't protocol. Grooms were laborers in the dust who weren't ever supposed to express an opinion about a horse to a trainer unless there was something obviously wrong with it.

When something was wrong, drugs were often used to deaden the horse's pain, but the legality around drugging varied from state to state. Except in New York, New Jersey, and Arkansas, a horse could run on Butazolidin—a well known anti-inflammatory. The problem with Bute was that it worked better on the horse than on the handicapper. Because the drug was legal—in controlled amounts—it wasn't necessary for the public to be informed which horses were on it, and some racetracks would opt for not listing the fact in the *Daily Racing Form.*

The tragedy of Bute was that, like any painkiller, it worked only as a mask—a shadow over evidence about the actual crisis. Bute or no Bute, a horse that was going to break down eventually did, and the ones who'd been drugged often enough would often be injured much more extensively than if they hadn't run on medication at all. The anti-inflammatory was known to make bones go soft, which sped up the horse's demise. If a cheap horse on Bute lived long enough, he'd dissolve.

Buddy used Bute on horses the same as any other trainer did, but it was Lasix, the wonder drug, that got trainers really excited. Lasix is a diuretic that also controls bleeding, and what's confusing about it is how the drug affects the horse that technically doesn't need it. For the non-bleeder, Lasix works to increase the production of urine and flushes away any traces of other drugs in the horse's system. It can cover the tracks of a mischievous trainer.

I wouldn't have called Buddy Fisk a mischievous trainer, but he was a gambler, which meant that any of his thorough-bred conditioning was intertwined with interests that weren't fully horse-minded. Buddy was trying to break even on a race-track that would never make him rich. The dreams here of any trainer were never as grand as they might have been on the Atlantic (Belmont Park) or the Pacific (Santa Anita). Mostly, the backstretch in Cincinnati, Ohio, was a conglomerate of barns run by men and women just trying to pay their feed bills.

But received through the senses, the racetrack was sultry and pungent. The smell of sweat from a horse after it worked three-eighths of a mile was unlike any other, and unlike my own, which was now mixed with sweet clover, vodka, nicotine, and timothy hay. The smell of tack (halters, bridles, saddles, and shanks), which poured out of the first room in the barn every morning as I walked down the shedrow, was a heady combination of oil soap, leather, and chalk. And heat. And later, in the afternoon, when I came back to feed, there was the luscious smell of bran and oats which the foreman had just mixed with hot water to make a mash. All those smells were thick with the present tense. Nothing bad could happen in a world that smelled like that or looked like that: a filly stand-ing like a statue with one leg bent back for the blacksmith, her eyes seemingly fixed on the brink of something, as if dreaming the morning workout back, but faster.

As strange as it felt initially, the racetrack put me in a kind of awe that made me instantly respect it. It was a world inside a world. Or maybe it was under the world, an allegory to a fable: a labyrinth of luck, into and out of which the horses I walked every day were leading me. But I was becoming bored with just walking horses and started reminding Richard of his promise that I'd be grooming soon—that he'd teach me how.

Late in the afternoons, after everyone else had left the barn in the lapse between dusk and dinner, Richard began to teach. He was a very serious teacher and had an intimidating sense of boundaries. I'd often try to make Richard laugh so that, in what seemed like the dizzy rapture of his work, he wouldn't forget that I was his lover.

"You have to feel for heat," Richard said. "Heat tells you a horse is hurting in the leg or in the ankle. Don't be afraid to run your hand down the front of his legs, but always be sure you're to the side of him. Never face him head on. He might strike."

And then Richard went back to the beginning, when morning got emptied—water buckets, hay racks, stalls—and the standing bandages wrapped the night before around the legs got removed. The bandages protected the legs if the horse got cast or thrashed around in the stall.

"Legs are the map to the treasure. The whole crazy business is built around a horse's leg," Richard said with importance.

Through Richard's teaching and a good word to Jewel, I soon got three horses to rub—none of which amounted to much, except for Over Pond, who might have been something but was as yet unproven. Buddy must have thought the horse would turn into something, though. Over Pond was always first on the list scrawled in lipstick or eyebrow pencil on the envelope that Jewel pulled out of her purse every morning. The list told us which horses were going out to the track and in what order. The more promising runners in the barn went first.

Every twenty minutes or so, a horse was led out of the stall fully dressed for the track: saddle cloth, saddle, and bridle. A horse prepared for work like this always took my breath away—something about the look in his eye. He wasn't posing, although there was a trace of that, like heat, in the gesture. But even more, he seemed to be listening to something far away and with the look was bringing it in. The whole move said he was in tune with something we humans could never hear or see. A horse looking at you straight on is never as thrilling, somehow. He isn't really looking at you because his eyes are so far apart. He's actually looking around you, I suppose. *You* are in the way.

After the horse took a few turns around the barn, the exercise boy would get up on him. The rider stepped into my hand, which in one reflexive hoist would put him in the saddle. *Leg up!* The rider was on, taking the horse out of the barn. The self that the grip of a hand could feel was all I got of the rider, but a horse got more. With a boy on his back, the horse had a way to feel time, broken up into athletic seconds on a silver stopwatch being stopped and started again by the trainers observing from the reviewing stand. I used to see them on my days off—the huddled circle of trainers at River Downs—watching their horses work, maybe for the first time, yelling down to the jock or the exercise person to let the reins out a notch, draw the reins in.

I could see Neil Howard (who'd later go on to train Summer Squall, a Kentucky Derby winner) and Chuck Coatney, Richard's father. I could see how nobody was talking, only looking far out across the track to where their charges were now galloping down the backstretch, getting ready to put it all into a next gear. It was public and private at once—the morning desire of a trainer.

While the horses were at the track, I cleaned out the feed tubs and water buckets and filled hay racks again and topped off the stalls with fresh straw. There was nothing like a freshly bedded stall, or what the morning light did to it. Vermeer found the light in painting when he made it stream through an open window: it could all be falling on this manger. Shaking out the straw made the softest sound in the shedrow—up in the treble clef, if you were orchestrating racetrack work. The rest of the music would be in the bass clef: water streaming into a bucket, the occasional guttural purr of pigeons whose nests I had to uproot to get the bales of straw down from the hayloft they'd be winging in.

A joke or a song might have turned in the morning air from some of the other grooms like Willie Bright or Jimmy Love, but we were in a hurry when the horses were out and would let the joke or the song float over our heads without response. The stalls had to be ready by the time the horses returned—winded and damp, needing a sponge bath or water from the hose, if they wouldn't stand still. A good horse liked his work. A cheap horse, in pain ninety percent of the time, only bore it.

After the bath, standing now with the horse in his stall, I

took the hard brush and the curry comb and rubbed the horse from the withers down to the stifle. I imagined I was rubbing light into him, and this made me feel there was only the present tense to think about. I rarely conjured up the past when I stood next to a horse; it wasn't there, but along with the emphasis on *now* was the potential danger I was facing whenever I groomed—the possibility that a horse could suddenly strike or bite me. I had to connect with the animal only now—nothing as far back as a past. Sometimes I had a hard brush in one hand, a soft one in the other and backed up one hard stroke with one soft—major to minor, a light went on, a light went off, like the light in a child's bedroom after the prayer to God not to take his soul while he sleeps. I'd get a dull cramp in my hands when I did this and would have to take a break from all the rigor I'd put into the brushing.

After the body came the legs, and I rubbed those with plain alcohol, or alcohol mixed with liniment—usually Absorbine or Beagle Oil, which some racetrackers used to strain through white bread to separate the alcohol from the fragrance so they could drink it. Then I wrapped clean white cotton and wrapped that again with flannel standing bandages. It was the best part of the grooming job because I was looking up now, awed by stature—my mind gone somewhere else down a corridor of silence.

I ran the cottons from the ankle, inside each leg, up to just below the knee. The bandages had to be tight enough to stay on, and then were fastened with steel bandaging pins. Richard taught me that if the bandages were wound too tight, a horse could "bow." The leg from the knee down to the ankle would fill up with fluid between the ligament and the cannon bone, causing a bowed tendon.

The last bit of ritual before I left the stall was the easiest and the best one for the horse—removing his halter. So many horses got feisty at this stage. They felt good. Their legs felt good under them. They were finished with me—the feely, talking blond animal.

Four
_____

First Race, First Dream

One day, Willie Bright left Mistress Mine alone for a minute while he ran to get some rubbing alcohol. As soon as he was halfway down the shedrow, the filly pulled the screw-eye out of the wall, ducked under the rubber stall guard that kept her in, and proceeded to bolt through the barn.

"Loose horse!" Willie Bright warned everyone. And we all laughed because we all used to say that Willie was such a loose horse himself. Without a halter to grab onto.

Mistress Mine was in the eighth race that day, and her tearing off down the shedrow could have been disastrous for the filly: something as minor as a nicked ankle or worse and she'd have to be scratched from the race. We caught her soon enough, though, coaxing her back to her stall with some loose hay we'd gathered while running to catch her. Since it was the first time a horse from our barn was actually in a race, Richard and I would be making our first trip over to the grandstand, too. It was an important trip for us—venturing out into the public beyond the backstretch or Bill's Bar. I bought a *Daily Racing Form* that morning and Richard showed me how to read it.

"The *Form* tells you everything. Don't bet on anything until you talk to me first, okay?"

"Yeah, sure. How much should I bet on Mistress Mine?" The talk around the outfit was that she was a pretty good filly, but she was running on the grass for the first time, so there was really no telling what she would do.

"We have to see how she ran in the mud," Richard said. "A good mudder will run good on the grass a lot of the time."

When we got to the races the crowd was rushing over to the betting windows to wager on the first race. The grandstand was glassy and impersonal, like a stock exchange inside a tunnel—nothing like the way it looked from a distance. Richard took out the *Daily Racing Form,* and I bought two beers. We sat down on a bench that looked out at the track.

There was something unsettling about being at the grandstand. I suppose it was being in public again, but more than just that crowd of dreamers was making me uneasy. I was in public in middle America—a place I never saw myself living in. What was I doing in Cincinnati? For the first time since hitting the racetrack, I missed New York.

"She looks good. She liked the mud when she ran on it. Bet twenty dollars on her."

Richard showed me how to read across the small type in the *Daily Racing Form* that looked like a phone book's and down each column that described all the factors of a horse's past performance: track condition, weather, size of field, purse, post position, jockey, order of finish.

"Consistency, class, trainer, and track condition—those are your main considerations," Richard said matter-of-factly. "Never bet on favorites."

"Why not? Don't they win most of the time?"

"Well, sure. But you won't make any money that way. You have to take a risk when you bet."

We had seven races to sit through before Mistress Mine was led out of the paddock. You can tell a lot about a horse in the paddock. It's the only chance you have to see a runner up close—whether it's nervous or calm, dry or "washed out" (broken out in a heavy sweat). A washed-out horse usually runs a washed-out race, having expended all its energy before the saddle's been put on.

After the paddock, the horses are taken down to the track and into a post parade where they're led in front of the grandstand only to be turned back again and loaded into the starting gate. Richard and I stood very still at the rail, looking at Mistress Mine: how she was traveling; how Charlie Woods, the jockey, was letting her have her head. He was sitting easy on top of her.

Passenger or pilot? This was what the racing crowd often asked when judging a jockey's performance. Either the jockey was working the horse, or the horse was working the jockey. It was a hard distinction to make when watching the actual race, but in the slowness of the post parade, the jockey seemed like he could only be a passenger.

And they're off!

Mistress Mine took the early lead and never looked back. All the other horses went by in a streak of colored silk. The jockeys sat upright, but as they got closer to home, they leaned down, more on the horses' withers, and sometimes hit the horse with a crop through the final furlong. The drive was thrilling. The track announcer's voice became emphatic. Erotic, even, sexy and fast.

"How does the track announcer remember the names of all the horses?" I asked Richard.

"He's memorized which silk color corresponds to which horse."

While the announcer's voice stayed pitched on ecstasy, the crowd's enthusiasm was more cadenced. Nobody cheered until the horses made that final turn for home. It was then that a fan would suddenly find his or her own voice and urge on the bet until the horse passed under the wire—the voice turning under a wave into joy or dread.

The first sound after the cheering stopped was always much softer: the tearing up of tickets. Some people who won at the races were very deliberate about their little victories and moved quietly toward the windows after a race to collect their money. And some were hysterical—not used to winning, I suppose. However they sounded, most of them looked the same on every track I ever worked: ethnically diverse, mostly middle-aged men, simply dressed. Working stiffs, I suppose. In the years I worked the track, I never met or talked to any of them. They were a group gathered around odds. What could I say? I could comprehend odds in those early days only when they were even—double your money. Even odds was easy math.

Mistress Mine went off at 10 to 1.

"How could she go off at odds like that, Richard? She won easy. I don't get it."

"Well, it was her first time on the grass. You never know."

I actually kissed Richard on the mouth after we collected our winnings. I'd kissed him in public before, plenty of times—we were drunks from New York, after all. But it felt strange kissing my lover at a racetrack in middle America.

There were horses in the kiss.

Horses were falling through time—through the road-dust and radios playing, through early nights of beer drinking and card playing in the kitchen. They were falling through late nights, when all the track was dark blue sky and barn light, falling through hay and rolling through straw.

That whole summer, horses were falling in my dreams. But the horse that would lead me into the paddock on the first Saturday in May was waiting to be born. Seth Hancock, owner of Claiborne Farm in Paris, Kentucky, was thinking of breeding Seattle Slew to a mare called Tuerta. The thought was falling through the owner's fitful sleep. What would a foal by 1977's Triple Crown winner amount to? He didn't know what to call it then, but it was Derby fever keeping that millionaire awake.

Five

After the First Death

My mother's death and its aftermath was the bell that sent me out of a gate in New York and put me onto the track for the race into Cincinnati. She called me the day before she died to tell me she was in crisis.

"I'm at the end of my rope," my mother said. "I'm going to change the locks on the front door to keep your stepfather out." My stepfather was hitting a dangerous and wavy phase in his manic depression—acted out as mental and physical abuse towards her.

Kathryn Jacqueline Osterman was the funniest and most tragic woman I ever knew. When she was in a particularly silly mood, she spoke in character voices, and all her letters to me at college were signed with other people's names. Nikita Khrushchev and Zelda Fitzgerald wrote to me often, and at that age, it didn't occur to me that my mother may not have wanted to be herself very much; she was just being funny. My mother also insisted that my brother and I never call her Ma or Mom—that if we didn't want to call her Kathryn, we could always just call her Sam.

But her sense of humor was always fighting with her life-long battle with depression, brought on initially by the death of her mother. Together, they had rented a house on Fire Island one summer and had a serious argument over a boy they both loved. The day after returning to the city at season's end, my grandmother jumped out the window onto Park Avenue, killing herself—a tragedy that her whole life my mother believed was caused by their one and only argument.

"Your grandmother was a Ziegfeld Follies girl, you know, and men would stop in the middle of the street just to look at her—she was that beautiful," my mother told me. "And she was in the movies. She was a chorus girl in *The Gay Divorcée* and danced on a white piano in *Gold Diggers of 1933*. Or was it the other way around?"

The show business stories my mother told me kept me enthralled (Alfred Hitchcock was interested at one time in making a movie about my grandfather, a song-and-dance man, and when my grandmother wasn't dancing on white pianos, she was Perry Como's secretary). But my favorite grandmother story evoked the New York of the early twenties, when vaudeville was king and many of its stars were wonderful eccentrics with decidedly different ideas on child-rearing.

"I brought my friend Barbara home from school one afternoon and there was my mother, naked in bed, with the sheet pulled up to her neck and a book in her hand, which she happened to be reading upside down. Barbara was practically hypnotized. But that wasn't enough—my mother was also sporting a sweet little beret on top of her head and a hand-drawn mustache over her upper lip."

"What did you do?" I asked, when I finally stopped laughing.

"Well, I introduced my mother to Barbara and she said, 'Bonjour, Barbara.' And Barbara? All she could say was that she didn't know my mother was French."

As close as the stories made me feel to my mother, I felt nothing but betrayal by the time the sex with my stepfather had gotten habitual. I sensed my mother knew what was happening and I resented her for not trying to put a stop to it. As emotionally mixed-up as the whole experience with my stepfather was and as much as I kept blaming myself for being its instigator, I secretly longed for an outsider to recognize it—to change the compulsive, dreamlike world the sex threw me into. But my mother was incapable of putting any energy into anything beyond what directly affected her: a marriage built on shaky ground. My guardians might never have gotten together in the first place were it not for coincidental nervous breakdowns.

In 1964, my mother and stepfather-to-be were admitted to Gracie Square Hospital suffering from nervous breakdowns. He'd recently been dumped by a girlfriend and became enamored with my mother for reasons that were never very clear to my brother, Kevin, and me. Upon discharge, my mother announced to the head nurse: "He wants to marry me—what do you think?" The nurse replied: "I don't think that's such a good idea, Kathryn, dear. He doesn't like women."

Which, of course, was true. My stepfather always liked telling the story about how he and a boy who later became a famous museum curator seduced each other on a camping trip one weekend when they were both students at Horace Mann. Years later, when I finally met the man at a garden party in Provincetown and told him who I was, he said, "Well, honey, I could have been your father!"

When my mother was released from the hospital, she asked Kevin and me if she should marry him. We were reading an Alfred Hitchcock story for kids about a grisly camping trip and I suppose I should have looked up from the lurid tale before giving her such an unconditional yes.

Soon after the marriage, my stepfather started saying things to hurt my mother—digs about her being overweight or about her addictive pill-taking. I remember a particularly horrible scene when we were living on Twelfth Street. From the dark hall I could see into my parents' bedroom, where my stepfather had laid my mother's purses out on a coffee-colored velour bedspread and was rifling through them, looking for drugs. He scooped the variously colored pills up furiously and flushed them down the toilet.

I was mad at them both—mad at my mother for not wanting to live, and mad that my stepfather had to make such a concerted effort to make sure that she would. I was confused by the scene and wondered when they had ever been friends. It seems to me now that whatever love my stepfather may have had for my mother had dissolved in a fog of mistrust and narcissism early on. He truly felt that she was doing this to him personally.

If alcohol was the mercurial hinge that kept Richard and me together, mental illness hinged my parents in an even more concrete way. And more desperately. They kept trying to save each other without ever knowing how to care for themselves as individuals. He was gambling, overeating, and behaving compulsively, particularly around money (he'd make little towers of loose change on top of the dresser every night, among other things). And she tried to kill herself at least twice in the fifteen or so years of their marriage.

One night, my stepfather discovered my mother nearly comatose on the bedroom floor. She had taken an overdose of sleeping pills, so he took her to the hospital. Although I don't remember what hospital or whether I visited her, I do know that it happened. And I remember that they stayed together a while longer, on medication and in and out of therapy. Eventually, I began to lose interest in them and started going my own way.

Self-realization by default.

It was in that default zone that I had my first drink. After a dinner party, I took the red wine that remained in several smeared glasses, poured it into a mug, and drank it.

The day before she died, my mother was supposed to meet Kevin for lunch. But Kevin never showed up because he was faltering, too—drunk and homeless and bitter, wandering the Bowery. I was an alcoholic by then, but I had Richard who kept saving me from the street, from self-harm, from coming face to face with the drinking.

"There's nothing you can do about Kevin," I said to my mother on the phone. "He can't hear you."

The next day I found a note stuck in my mailbox. It was from a cousin: "Call me," it said. "It's urgent."

"It's your mother, she's . . ."

"She's what? What happened?"

"This isn't the kind of thing you tell someone over the phone."

I was in shock. I knew my mother was dead, but I couldn't believe I was having this conversation.

"Your mother died this morning. Of a heart attack, they think."

I drank everything left in the apartment and called Richard. He was in Ohio painting his millionaire father's house for some money and never enough love. Or was it love and never enough money? I broke through the busy signal. Richard arrived on the next plane out of Cincinnati.

On the night my mother was buried, my lover and I had a kind of sex we'd never had—passionate to the point of violence. We moved from the bedroom into the bathroom, into the living room, biting down on each other's hands, pulling each other's hair. At one point we were both actually leaning out the window. The fact that I hadn't seen Richard in some time certainly added to the quality of the sex, but there was something about mortality in it, too, as though the knowledge of death had come closer to us and Richard and I were compensating for its inevitability by acting as if we were superhuman.

On the morning of my mother's death, I'd been listening to water. I had followed someone through the after-hours bars to the river down at the end of Christopher Street.

At approximately two o'clock that same afternoon, Kevin wandered from downtown on the Bowery uptown to Riverside Drive, where he was picked up by the cops for trying to disassemble a Rolls-Royce. The cops took him to Roosevelt Hospital for observation. Then he was transferred to Manhattan State, where he wore sunglasses with one of the lenses missing and balanced a crumbled straw hat on his head—a kind of Clyde Barrow-Truman Capote mix.

In Brooklyn, at approximately ten o'clock in the morning, my stepfather went for a walk and checked himself into Downstate Hospital. Something was wrong with his mind, but he didn't know what it was. "I need a rest," he told the nurse at the front desk. New York is probably the only city in the world where someone could walk into a hospital and be admitted after saying something like that.

While none of us knew anything yet, the family was behaving strangely that day—floating in space the morning my mother died, acting out unusual little scenes in a world that was different for us, though we didn't know it yet.

Six

Second Dream

My mother's death was the only cloak from New York that I was still wearing, and it provided the only clue to my real identity; I would have been rendered invisible without Richard there to see me. Or Buddy and Jewel Fisk, for that matter. The daily regimen of hard work around racehorses made me visible in my bosses' eyes too, I suppose. The more I did it, the more I knew who I was among horses. Because the work, after all, was specialized.

And because those Fisk horses were cheap and in pain so much of the time, the work of "holding" them (keeping them sound) would often change. Where alcohol on the legs might be effective one day, the next day those same legs might be carrying heat and would have to be done up in mud or poultice. Frisky Flyer was a filly like that. Her legs were in a constant state of change, like odds on a toteboard in those last harried minutes before the horses are sprung from the starting gate.

One morning Buddy Fisk entered Frisky Flyer in a race she should have won laughing. The filly had scored her last out and was being dropped in price because she was sore. Buddy wanted to get rid of Frisky this time, so she was running for a tag ($7,500 and she's yours). Taking a horse like Frisky (she'd won her last out in allowance company) was a pretty sound investment—on paper, anyway.

"Be sure you boys freeze her legs, now. And for chrissakes, don't leave that blister on for too long," Buddy commanded Richard and me before going over to the grandstand that afternoon. Frisky was actually my horse, but Buddy never fully acknowledged that I was grooming now. I'd joked with Richard that the fact of his being my lover was something Buddy probably figured was enough of a job.

Freezing required icing and the application of a blistering compound to the front part of the leg every half hour or so. Critical to the whole procedure was being sure not to rub the compound in or leave it on for too long because the skin could simply peel off. Everything looked good until the race actually went off. Poor Frisky came down the stretch in terrible pain; it looked as if she were running on eggshells. Apparently, the compound hadn't been removed soon enough and the filly's legs were starting to blister. Buddy was furious—his horse didn't win, and he'd bet his lungs on her.

And I'd failed. But a door opened. In my anger, I was able to turn away from the horse I'd had to work so hard on in order to get her to run. What had once felt humbling and self-forgetting suddenly seemed useless to me. I realized that afternoon that I no longer wanted to take cripples over to the grandstand. Or, at the very least, to be responsible for Frisky's trouble—jamming up the quick fix that was supposed to push the filly over the finish line.

I quit the Fisk outfit and went to work six stables over. A trainer named Kim Green had her hands on a runner named Star of Monaga and needed a groom. Kim hired me on the same day I quit Buddy and Jewel. She'd heard I was queer, which was a ticket into the barn, I think. Kim was a lesbian—the only one I knew of on the track—and hiring me, I'd joke with her later, was just a way of keeping it in the family.

Richard was much less bent on the illusion of success on the racetrack than I was. He wished me well with Kim and Star of Monaga, but he'd always loved the work for itself alone, not for any money or power one imagines when laying his or her hands on the legs of a priceless thoroughbred star. Something in the tone of Richard's good wishes told me that his love for horses was winning out over what love he had for me, which I might have anticipated had I arrived at the races with a clearer head. There was a quality about returning home to the landscape of horses, and a father in the vicinity, that was bound to change Richard back into the person he was before

I ever entered his life. He wasn't running blindly when he'd left New York and me in a stupor. Richard knew that by running to horses, he'd thrive in a way he could never thrive in New York.

And as if I had suddenly taken leave of my body and could see this whole scene with more objectivity, I realized *I'd* been the one chasing Richard. I couldn't get it into my head at the beginning that Richard had left *me,* and no countermove on my part would ever change the intention of that original act. Richard wasn't planning to see me again, and the fact that I had followed him may have been . . . what? Flattering? Maybe at first, but it was also confusing. My presence kept Richard's leaving me from ever being the definitive gesture he'd intended it to be.

The needs of a horse were easier for Richard to meet now. And he could see results. While I'd thought we were trying the races out as a way to live better with each other, the environment was more spacious for my lover to be himself in. I realized, watching him grooming horses, that in a way I had backed him into a corner. I was an enigma in a world that now hinged on the shining coat of a two-year-old colt or eight races in the afternoon. And while Richard still acknowledged me, it was the way one simply acknowledges a piece of one's history— a crease in a map of a journey. I had been part of his life, but he didn't need me as much in his newer one.

Richard started spending more time in the stalls. Even on the afternoons when he didn't have to work, or on his days off, I would find him with Ax by Ex (a filly coming up on her first race) in her stall, packing her feet with mud, talking to her.

And while it may have been important to the filly, it was also a time for Richard not to have to deal with me—the other unknown quantity. He couldn't have known what Ax by Ex would do her first race, but at least he could participate in getting her there. With me, and with every upcoming, unpredictable drunk, Richard couldn't take part.

As far back as 1972, when I first met Richard, my alcoholism was a place I inhabited by myself, and as much as there was the pull of desire toward my lover (from that first summer day when we met), there was and would continue to be the alcohol pull, too, which had nothing to do with human love. Richard and I were opposites, physically and mentally, making our relationship so interesting right from the beginning. I've never understood the narcissistic component to some gay lives whereby one ends up with his double. I'm attracted to my opposite, not entirely without some of the same physical characteristics as my stepfather: short, dark hair, hirsute. But Richard was another animal altogether.

He was a bartender then and the most adamant dreamer I'd ever met. Nothing that he wanted to happen in his life was there yet. What made Richard the dreamer I fell in love with was the fact that his dreams—artistic aspirations, mostly—sounded as if they could actually make him a better person. And then they became about us and the rest of our lives together, dreams that started when we were both still awake and finishing each other's sentences.

The glitch with Richard was that he was involved with two other people at the same time: Carlos and Bernard, two very hot Latin guys. I paled beside them, at least physically. I didn't look too bad—I was a nineteen-year-old on a mostly liquid diet, after all—but I didn't have a gym body. I wasn't really conscious of having a body. While I felt the two men in Richard's life were no match on a mental and spiritual plane—the only planes I seemed to live on—I knew they were powerful sex partners for Richard. There was no way I could compete with that kind of prowess. It just wasn't available to me, the way it is to some men. I had to locate it first, under a vibration of self-consciousness.

I don't know what I did exactly to "win" Richard, but I found myself in the emotional swirl of a chase. I was pursuing him, leaving my own life and entering his life, about which I knew very little. Ultimately, I did win him. I must have sweet-talked Richard and given him enough space, too. Something in the experiment of pursuit succeeded. But there was a part about getting together that didn't feel strategic at all. Our love for each other from the very beginning felt too fated to fail.

I first tested the love with a call to Richard from a pay phone one morning after I'd left a puzzle ring at his apartment. I asked him if I could come over and pick it up, that I wanted to see him again, that I already knew I liked him a lot. He liked me too, but his previous involvements worried me and I wanted to talk to him about them. He told me that he was certainly more attracted to me than to Carlos or Bernard, but he would need time to part from each of them with any kind of grace. I gave him two weeks (an uncharacteristically aggressive demand on my part), and in that time he not only left the two relationships but asked me to move in with him during a frenzied weekend when he went off to Fire Island for something called the Bartender Awards.

The apartment had a bathtub in the kitchen and a pink baby grand piano in the living room. The woman we bought the piano from had once taken a can of Comet to its white-and-gold-leaf trim, which probably accounted for the piano's being for sale in the first place. The space could hold little else but that piano and a big brass bed, which we later traded so I could take voice lessons. We traded the bed because money was always precarious for both of us—arriving in windfalls that would last for only a while. The bed assured the future of my voice—for the next two years, anyway.

The walk-up was filled with an assortment of wonderful and diverse characters. Many of the tenants were ushers at the Broadway houses—middle-aged to older, plain-speaking women whom I remembered from every Saturday afternoon as a child, when they would take me down the aisle of a movie palace. How important they were to me! No matter how scary some of those movies were, these women made me feel safe. Their presence in the aisle meant that darkness was only temporary—a condition that lasted only as long as the images moving across an ocean of occupied screen.

On the afternoons when there was no matinee, the ushers from Hell's Kitchen sat on fluffy pillows in their windows and yelled across the courtyard to each other. As loud and insistent as all that chatter was, I felt a great sense of calm inside it—the simple and loving hum of humanity, like listening to baseball, low on the television, when you're falling asleep.

But one morning in 1977, Richard and I decided to move.

We were tired of the bathtub in the kitchen. There wasn't enough space, and the rooms were "too small to hold the feelings we have for each other," Richard said one night before falling asleep. We deserved more and had some money too, so a move was actually possible (it would never be again). After only a week, we found an apartment on Seventy-ninth Street between Broadway and Amsterdam. It had a beautiful bay window in the bedroom and a huge living room with a working fireplace. Richard sanded the floors and after we sold the pink piano for double what we'd paid for it (Richard refinished it), we bought another one. My job was to get the kitchen together—an experiment in terra-cotta wall paint and limited shelving. I also put up the photographs and paintings we had between us—a decorative move on my part that was startling to both of us. I had no aesthetic for interiors.

Our first guest in the new apartment was a photographer who was famous for taking pictures of naked men stranded in demolished rooms and relating erotically to some prop, usually a toy. In those strangely nonsexual portraits, a man sans accoutrements was an image of despair. Still, I had been a longtime admirer of the photographer's work and was excited when he agreed to take our pictures.

But the shoot was uncomfortable for various reasons. I didn't like the man very much and he kept wanting Richard and me to pose with full erections, which we wouldn't do. The one photograph that made it into a book some years later was of Richard and me hunched up under the window shutter in our bedroom, naked and looking terrified. I can't remember if the photographer had given us a "motivation"—that awful term—to respond to while gazing into his glass eye, but we certainly didn't look too happy about being recorded on film. We looked like two stowaways on a frigid ship.

There was another photograph from the session that made it into a copy of *Mandate* magazine, the most popular gay porno publication at the time. It was a photograph of Richard—naked, of course—standing with a saxophone around his neck. I'm in a very high swivel chair, clothed, with my arm down as far as it will go into the horn's opening. What was odd about the photo (it was used as a spread to accompany the magazine's record reviews) was the fact that for some strange reason the photographer or the magazine had decided to airbrush Richard's penis out of it. There was no gender-bending consciousness whatsoever in those days; the image evoked the same effect as a Diane Arbus photograph—the viewer was engaged and confused at once. I was mad at the photographer and felt awful for Richard. But Richard didn't seem to mind not having a penis.

In retrospect, it seems that for the short time we lived on Seventy-ninth Street, Richard and I lived well. We had extraordinary Christmases (fur coats, kitchenware, cameras, books, records, silk robes) and then for some reason, we stopped demonstrating our love. We just had it. Of course, we were "used" to love and whether it was the physical beauty we saw in each other wearing off or if it was everything that made us true opposites starting to push us further and further apart, I'm not sure. Most plausibly, it was the affair each of us was having separately with alcohol. We were each steadily sinking in New York's glamor and recklessness—after-hours bars, bathhouses, transvestite clubs, and cabarets. Not that any of those places necessarily made the soul weary, but they were not healthy rooms for me because they always collaborated with my will to disengage.

Alcohol was getting behind drunken attacks Richard and I launched on each other, and I'd become more and more maudlin and self-destructive. I kept threatening to kill myself for no good reason in particular. It was just an excuse to be able to whirl through the kitchen wielding a frying pan. My mother's death that year was a vague reason I said I'd do myself in, but Richard knew better. He knew that self-pity was the liquor talking, which made him apathetic, finally, as far as my state of mind or even physical safety was concerned.

One night in particular so worried me that I felt its horrible sequence of events pull at the deeper fabric of the relationship. I couldn't function for days afterwards. For the first time, Richard had succeeded in scaring me. I'd been drinking alone and had stopped off at the corner delicatessen for a sandwich to take home with me. As usual, I had forgotten to eat dinner. I'd been to hear Robert Kraft and the Ivory Coast at the Village Gate earlier in the evening. When I went through the front door of the walk-up, I was grabbed from behind by a thug. He dragged me upstairs to the apartment and forced me to open the door. It was dark inside except for a little light far down the hall coming from the kitchen that indicated Richard was probably home.

While the attacker pulled me into the kitchen and put a knife to my throat, Richard sat up in the loft bed and looked down at me, smoking a cigarette, shaking his head. He looked dumbfounded and took a puff on the cigarette each time the drunken thug would utter something, mostly gibberish. After releasing me, finally, the thug grabbed the stereo equipment and a television on the way out—usual snares from a random crime like this one.

I'd never been angrier with Richard or more mystified. While we'd had our share of alcohol-devised danger, it had always involved just the two of us. The abuse toward each other, silent or hysterical, would flare and pass and then become a quality in the relationship, but never enough to indicate we were headed for real trouble. This was an outside danger I had brought into the kitchen, and as drunk as I may have been, the assault seemed like something that would have happened no matter what state I was in. The guy would have grabbed the next sucker walking through the door. Still, I hated Richard's indifference.

A week later I realized Richard's behavior wasn't exclusively a reaction to me. He was suffering privately, too. One night I found him sitting on a stoop on Forty-sixth Street, crying into his hands, not knowing who I was. Drunk. When I asked Richard to come home with me, he threatened to kill himself and said it in a way only a drunk can—finding words for the moment when the world is more believable as a metaphor:

"There's a bridge in my mind I'm going to jump from," he said.

In a way, Richard did jump, but it took longer than that one night for him to land in Cincinnati. He jumped into the barn, and while he was working for the Fisks and I was with Kim Green now, we still slept together, even though our barns were far apart. Sex was all that was keeping us interested in each other, it seemed. We hadn't drifted totally apart yet, but if you had asked me then what was keeping me tethered to Richard, however loosely, I would have said it was his arms around me every once in a while. I would have said Richard made it so that I didn't have to wake up alone in the middle of so many horses.

Seven

Stars

When Juan yelled out "Star!" to me one morning after I'd been with Kim Green for a couple of weeks, he wasn't talking to me but referring to a horse. In that moment I had become fully known to Juan without ever having to say a word. Star of Monaga and Michael Klein were one, like Wallace Stevens's blackbird in its thirteen worlds, and we were a horse Juan knew could run.

She was one of the fastest fillies in Ohio; very few horses

could beat Star of Monaga going six furlongs. The day she won over Donny Rowe's "big" horse, Grand Time, was a turning point for the Green outfit. Having a big horse made a job on the track much more tolerable, and it was the first time I felt I was moving toward something other than just a weekly paycheck. Having a big horse was like dropping the future into a wishing well.

And Star kept winning. The victories brought me out of that early hypnosis I'd fallen under in the cathedrallike barn that now I realized had given me a skewed view. Underneath the romance of talking to animals and waking up in moonlit mornings sparsely populated by oldtimers was the harder fact of what success on the track really was. The dewy-eyed look of the beginner was dissolving in me. If I could keep the drinking under control (not every day, not as much, only at night), I could turn this into something like a career—my least favorite word up until then. I grew up believing that having a career was the downfall of any real artist. An artist doesn't want a career; he wants a mission.

The day Star of Monaga buried Grand Time, I walked her to the spit box, the post-race blood and urine testing area where a horse was checked for drugs and the only place in the world where you had to whistle to get a winner to piss. As soon as the filly watered off, one of the crew was called over and ducked into the stall to collect her urine with a ten-foot-long pole that had a glass jar in the holder at the end: a wand, I imagined, to cast a spell that filled the jar.

"Not her again. Jee-suz Christ," moaned the piss collector.

"Yessir," I grinned, knowing well the drill reported to me

by Kim. Star of Monaga wouldn't piss. Ever. We always had to wait two days for the blood test to come back, so she was a filly who never officially won any of her races until they were remembered—a trick in time that made all her win pictures records of the most favorable conditions and not actual fact.

When I passed Neil Howard's barn, Jimmy, Howard's assistant trainer, congratulated my filly and me on a job well done.

"I never thought you'd beat that thing of Rowe's," Jimmy offered with an enchanted disbelief that came in the same look that shivered once through a man in Truro, Massachusetts, when I was eighteen. The look was a shiver because it was made of magnetism—what I remember as the first stare from a man that I could safely call a pass. I was thrilled to the point of speechlessness that long-ago summer: Finally! Someone knows I'm a homosexual.

"Well, I guess that horse had his mind on something other than running today. He's a good one, though," I said in an uncharacteristic flurry of track jargon. I was being kind, too— uncritical, it occurs to me now, because my horse had just won and I was lightheaded. Tinsley's Hope, Rising Profits, and Leader Jet were just three of the horses that were faster than Grand Time, but Rowe's horse had run with all of them by then already, so I was confident that Star of Monaga had just beaten a horse with class. And Green was beaming, for a change.

My new boss was a pretty serious character. She didn't seem to like the work very much and arrived at the barn each morning as if she were waltzing into a bank. In a way, she was.

I got along with Kim because I was indebted to her for giving me a horse like Star, but Green was in a bad mood most of the time. It would be easy, and in those days typical, to say that she didn't like men because she was a lesbian, but I don't think she liked horses all that much either. She also had a very strange lover who spent most of the time in the tack room they lived in together. I would see the girlfriend every once in a while when the door was left open, frying up a catfish on the hot plate and rocking in a huge wicker chair that took up most of the room.

Queers didn't rise to the surface too readily in the eclectic mix of racetrack types (except in New York, where there were simply more of them). It may be because we were so few that we were tolerated at all, or that our otherness was so marginal that it didn't qualify for outright bias, but I also think it was because queer fell under the same heading most racetrackers themselves fell under: outsider.

Empathy was reserved for racehorses, and there wasn't a great deal of it left over for the outsider. We were all marginal: dreamers and drunks in the barns. What made you marginal in the bigger world—race or sexual preference, for instance—got left at the racetrack gate, like a horse's breeding sometimes got left at the starting gate, a euphemism to explain why a well-bred horse could turn in a bad performance. The outsider, or anyone else for that matter, didn't merit a gaze. There was only one deep well of attention here: the horse, the horse, the horse.

When the gaze on the outsider did materialize, it was usually sexual, and when that happened there would suddenly appear dens of iniquity at River Downs to make the sex even more exotic: in a tack room on a mattress thrown under a horse blanket amidst the bridles and saddles, or up in the hayloft over the heads of twenty sleeping horses. Around this time, I had met Fran and was instantly drawn to him. Fran didn't know about Richard and I didn't tell him. He was a hot-walker who worked for another outfit, and he was coarse and angry and the sexiest kid I had met since leaving New York. He reminded me of the blond hustler I'd met on Eighth Avenue in New York who called himself Blue Diamond. Blue wouldn't have sex with me unless I paid him, which I didn't.

The idea of having sex with someone other than Richard seeped into me like a drug because it wasn't really an option until a physical body in the form of Fran presented itself. I didn't even know if Fran was gay, but we looked at each other a lot without saying anything, so the corridor seemed wide enough to dance through. I made a pass at him one night when we were in his barn after everyone else had left. Richard was drinking alone at Bill's Bar.

I put my hand on Fran's crotch, which now seems brusque but didn't then. It felt like what we both were trying to say. I asked him if he liked it.

"Yeah, I like that. I want that," Fran said, backing into an empty stall, pulling me along.

"I'm going to bury you now," I said, which as I said it sounded to me like a sudden switch in mood—lighter, less bent on having sex. I piled fresh straw over him with the same playful determination I showed a boyhood friend in the sand at Brighton Beach a thousand summers ago. Fran laughed and then got suddenly serious, as if what was going to happen was

happening for the first time and he had to make sure he wanted to go through with it. I let him make the first move. Then
he unzipped my fly. We were drinking from a bottle of Boone's
Farm apple wine.

I fucked Fran in a sudden rush of dominance, meshing
with the straw that kept taking us deeper into its world the
more we moved into each other and our drinking. And when
we were finished, when we were past the awkward, impulsive
glow, Fran couldn't say very much. He seemed to be having
regrets. I didn't say very much either, but I was thinking he
was a very hot kid. I didn't say "hot," of course. In life, I never
said hot. It was too pornographic. I said something like "beautiful." "Fran, I think you are beautiful," which was too formal
a thing to say to a farm kid. "Beautiful" must have sounded
odd to a boy who probably hadn't had a lot of homosexual sex.
It must have sounded vague.

Henry was the first instance of beautiful for me. In high
school we had been best friends. But I was thoroughly enamored of Henry and wanted to be more than just his friend. He
had long blond hair and a goatee and really did look like
Jesus—the image of Jesus on a paper fan I found in a thrift
shop.

We I used to pass notes to each other in history class—dis-
guised love poems that by the end of the week would merge
into something we'd collaborated on. Henry and I were falling
in love but didn't have a clue to what it was then. I fantasized
about having sex with him the whole time we were "friends"
but never let on how I really felt—perhaps a typical early battle with homosexuality. But my reluctance to say anything

wasn't because I was ashamed of being a homosexual. I was more ashamed of not being able to distinguish between friendship and love. Our friendship seemed like something to settle for, when what I really wanted was to sleep with Henry in the same bed.

One night in Brooklyn, after drinking two bottles of white wine and lying out together on my roof looking at the stars, Henry and I kissed for the first time and in the kiss was everything I had hoped was true about our relationship but hadn't yet been confirmed—that we were in love and the two of us were not just pals getting through a tough school together, listening to music, talking about girls and boys, driving aimlessly in a car now and then in search of life outside bleak Brooklyn.

It was a memorable night, but Henry and I were never able to be lovers. He liked having sex with women, too, and I think in the months that followed he felt my attraction to him wearing him down. Henry couldn't reciprocate my moves toward him any longer. With a serious girlfriend now, he'd crossed over to a place where homosexuality was strange to him—a reflex kick from the examining table after the doctor's rubber-hammer blow to the knee—strange to him, maybe, but still there. Physical.

What was so important about having my tongue inside Henry's mouth was how it finally substantiated what had before been shadowed by a stepfather's mystery role. The erotic life with my stepfather was so skewed and confusing and the abuse so ambiguous, I wasn't quite sure if it was the excitement of so many forces driving me at once or if I was afraid of his violence or if I really was a homosexual. What Henry's kiss did was give me the knowledge that I was beginning to like sex with a man for its sheer eroticism, not as a way to sedate the lover's body so it wouldn't get violent.

Fran didn't kiss, but he was still one of the reasons to stay at River Downs, which was quickly, by this time, revealing the paradoxes everybody knew existed but nobody ever talked about. The business felt improvisational because so much of it was dreamlike, but it was also repetitious and there were nagging practicalities that made the place undesirable. The pay was horrible, there was no health insurance, the food was from a parallel universe, and the hours seemed inhumane. And there was Commissioner Gabe.

Commissioner Gabe was as good a horse as there was around Ohio tracks, and he made a lot of money by local standards. The horse had won some stakes, and the day I saw him win the eighth race he broke the track record—running the six furlongs in 1:08 (1:12 was usual for Ohio). But breaking the record was fatal for Commissioner Gabe. He broke his leg after crossing the finish line and had to be destroyed. The track officials laid Gabe out on a mountainous manure pile because they didn't have enough sense or dignity to give him a proper resting place, and seeing that dead horse froze the track in time. River Downs was suddenly very clear and ordinary, a place I was visiting but didn't live in. The vision of Gabe, with the pulsing steam drifting like a spirit out of his body into the rainy afternoon sky, was a mean one. The racetrack had turned into a murder scene.

Gabe was the first dead horse I ever saw, even before a dead person (I never saw my mother's dead body). The sight of him, dull and heavy, made me think back to the first horses I ever saw up close. They weren't racehorses, of course, but fleabitten souls who wandered the dull green and hot hills of a day camp in Yonkers, New York, when I was eight years old. My brother and I rode those horses twice a week. The experience seemed like torture for me because it looked like such torture for the horses. They were sore and old and had lost everything down to the look in their eyes. They moved cautiously, as if the weight of even a child's imagination on a summer afternoon were too much for them to bear. I actually remember a day I was sitting on top of one of them, trying not to move around too much because I was sure the horse would buckle under me.

Two days after Commissioner Gabe died, Star of Monaga ran out of race conditions. Because she was a good horse by Ohio standards but not a great horse by history's standards, the only races left for her were stakes, which she could never win. So I left Kim Green and went crawling to Buddy and Jewel, who were more than happy to take me back. With Star of Monaga out of the picture, I flopped back to being merely mortal, and when Juan saw me in the track kitchen on a morning I was back living in my old life, out from under the shadow of a star, he didn't say hello. I'm sure Juan had forgotten my name.

Buddy and Jewel were headed to a racetrack called Beulah Park in Grove City, Ohio, as soon as the meet at River Downs was over, and Richard and I would go with them. Still, I couldn't understand why an outfit traveled to another track— interstate, yet—to run against basically the same company of horses. It was like changing laundromats. The purses were the same, the jockeys were the same, the food was the same. The only difference now was that Beulah Park had even worse living accommodations than River Downs did—thoroughly makeshift and with more concrete. And a town into which the main gate swung that was much nastier than Cincinnati. If there was ever a fag-basher lurking, he lurked in Grove City.

In that little town, Richard and I looked forward to simple pleasures like sex and eating, two activities at which we had become absolutely expert. We were having a kind of sex at the time that made us glow: in the hayloft, at midnight.

We were shadows in the straw when I was going into Richard and Richard into me. Before that, we were just two bodies in the room with the big oak table. My hands touched Richard's body and he laughed—because I am younger, I thought. Or because less light makes it more specific and there's something frightening about that and you laugh.

And I talked to him.

We kissed.

Then I drew my finger around his nipple and then with my tongue drew the circle that always took me back to Henry's nipple and the static on Henry's radio. Every time we ended up in Henry's bed after the perfunctory shower where we never looked at each other in the eye, he would turn on the radio above his head. It was as if he were bringing in the world outside, in order to make us listen harder to the one we were in: the one of moisture and peach fuzz and yellow light outlining Henry's long yellow hair.

Richard was this spring night's circle. We pulled sheets

around us like skirts and crept into the barn where we climbed the ladder the pigeons shat on and flung ourselves into bales of straw packed tightly in wire and stacked above the heads of twenty sleeping horses.

The hayloft at midnight.

This was where our shadows were, and where I was going into Richard and he was biting my neck going into me, and where I could claim the image of a struck match in all the drinking dark that hit upon a jewel in the bottom of drunkenness's hollow well—that I still had enough life in me that didn't have to swim the hard river of alcohol or get burned up by the dark. Enough life to have the jewel without swallowing it.

Often, we went down to the railroad tracks at night and, afterwards, ended up at the great Italian restaurant that was there. Still, I fantasized a lot, having entered the room that had once had Fran in it. I also fantasized because I was young, or so I kept rationalizing. I had met Richard when I was nineteen and had never really gone through the promiscuous period that was common to men my age.

In Grove City I fantasized about glowing with Nathan, who'd been through every racetrack in the Northeast as though they were detoxes. Nathan spoke in short, grunting sentences that were filled with humor and nicotine, and he touched his crotch a lot when he was talking, as if he were getting used to himself physically. Richard and I had a threesome with him one blurry night, but to this day, nobody remembers a thing. All I remember is Miles Davis's version of "Someday My Prince Will Come" and Nathan's dark blue workshirt with the ripped-out arms and safety pins for buttons.

Beulah Park was not racing's answer to Fort Knox. The outfit won only two races—just enough money in stakes to drink in a hostile bar for a couple of hours. Our time in Grove City felt like a segue to something else, but I didn't know what it was, until one morning before coffee, Jewel announced: "We're going to Latonia, boys!" Night racing. Even in this lower quadrant of the racing world, Latonia Racetrack was the worst plant in the East. Bargain racing. The horses there were put together with ice and painkillers and prayers to Eclipse, the foundation horse every thoroughbred leads back to.

The most dangerous thing in my life up to then happened at Latonia, which is why I remember the place at all. I was walking a horse called Aide to Reason, who spooked very easily. If there was a gum wrapper blowing in the breeze, it would absolutely shock him. This was not a good quality in a racehorse because it meant he would never be adequately prepared. Running in a race is a lot scarier than a gum wrapper. Aide to Reason finally did break his maiden, but we had to practically blind him. His right eye was actually patched so he couldn't see out of it.

In our walk around the barn something startled the big roan colt, and he bolted as if the barn were on fire and he had to run back into it, as horses will do. What was dangerous about the chase around the shedrow was that I didn't have the presence of mind simply to let go of the shank I was holding onto. I foolishly thought I could stop him in his eighty-mile-per-hour tracks. And though it's a funny story now, he could have kicked me in the head or pulled off my arm.

Most racehorses aren't dangerous, but occasionally there's

one that will kill you. One horse down in Hialeah, so the story goes, picked up a groom with his teeth—the groom's back was turned—and dragged him to the back of the stall and stomped him to death. And the champion John Henry was apparently ferocious, practically under lock and key whenever he was boarding at whatever racetrack he had been shipped over to run at.

The irony about John Henry was that the reason he was a gelding in the first place was because he was so mean. But losing his testicles didn't make him docile, it just made him angrier. It also made him the racehorse he was. This is the irony of gelding horses: it's done to make them what they are, to keep their minds on racing. The sexual mind in a colt can certainly make him a dull competitor—good news where a top filly is concerned. In general, boys can simply outrun fillies, but trainers will often run a good filly against the boys, and many times the filly will win. With the filly in front, a colt will often think about how he can enter her, not how he can pass by her.

Night racing at Latonia was harsh. The racetrack itself is in an armpit of American horse racing called Florence, which is a desolate outpost along an early stretch of Kentucky right after Cincinnati, if you're driving. It was a place I felt banished to for doing something wrong to horses. A rehab for grooms.

Night racing froze to my skin because sometimes it was below zero. And it always came after I'd been in the barn since early morning. All I wanted was to sleep for an hour, but it took at least that long to get a horse not worth the twenty dollars I was going to bet on him ready to run in what could have been the last race: Number nine, which went off at something like 11:30 P.M.

Then, after all that work, the horse would just lose again and tell me in eyes as empty as the pockets of an all-night gambler that he'd show me something next time. And I never knew if that was right. Any racehorse might have been something special. A race might have been coming up that made him special and turned him a certain way. That's why I worked so hard, because I never knew. It was all as haphazard and superstitious as the garlic I would see a year later at Hialeah, strung in garlands over each stall in José Rivera's barn: each wreath hung there like a Christmas in the country. Each an Argentine charm. A horse could turn into a star.

And sometimes it happened with a simple change in equipment, in the spirit of experimentation—an instruction to the jockey not to use the whip, put blinkers on the horse, tie the tongue down. Sometimes it happened when something inside the horse suddenly came forward: a change of heart, or the idiosyncratic hookup of each interval of strenuous training he'd spent so many just-after-sunrises in. The right race came up, a mob was cheering, the track was easy to grab, and he wanted to run.

Night racing began in a great darkness. And sometimes the horse broke down and I was reduced again to whatever it is in the human condition that jumps in front of hope. Another night, when I didn't have to work, I called it a kind of acquired loneliness—mute but still attentive—what felt like retrospect. But that night, in Kentucky, I knew it was solitude.

Old friend. Noble smoke among some barely visible stars. Vaguely noble.

Sometimes Richard and I got off the track and went to the Dark Horse bar where I played the jukebox—that reminder of a world singing, making money, going platinum without us. Aretha Franklin had a new song then: "Love All the Hurt Away." There was a lyric that said we had to *mend all the cracks in our hearts,* and as sophomoric as it sounded, I understood how the racetrack might have been a place for that mending to take hold, but drinking kept disconnecting the experience from any of its restorative power.

Being alcoholics trying to love each other, Richard and I were like two wounded birds—a recovering drunk would tell me years later—trying to make a nest. I was so inside my own alcoholism that I couldn't even see Richard's drinking. In part, I was hoping the red wine in a mug would help me find the hole in the ice I fell through during high school, when my drinking life began.

It was 1966 when everything happened first: incest, pills, secrecy, music too loud for my stepfather, my mother still in bed at three o'clock in the afternoon, a dog nobody wanted to walk, the growing circle of piss in the middle of the cheap living room rug because of it, stealing money out of my mother's purse and coat pockets, blender drinks, beers and shots, stealing speed out of my mother's purse, incest, reaching into my stepfather's underwear in the kitchen but not kissing him.

After this litany of circumstances which "anyone would drink over," I would later joke, my alcoholism progressed right along with the ability to recognize others like myself.

Alcoholics were a clan apart, like vampires, and I needed to see how they lived. I belonged to them. I was drinking to get out of the world, but there wasn't enough booze in the world to do it—the desert island of alcoholism.

But life would change. At the same time Richard and I were huddled over the jukebox in the Dark Horse, Tuerta was in foal to Seattle Slew. The horse that would change me—and Richard and me—was no longer just the dream that had been keeping Seth Hancock awake a whole year. Turning inside Tuerta's belly was a dark bay colt getting ready for light— about to cross over into all our waking lives.

Eight

Spoils of War

"Enough!" I announced, drunk, in front of our barn. "Hail, hail, Latonia," Richard sang loudly, conducting the imaginary orchestra with a beer bottle. We were sitting on a couple of empty poultice buckets, grabbing the beers from a muck basket we'd filled with ice, trying to figure out how we ever got to this flattened-out section of Kentucky—the perfect desolate setting to watch the last groom from the last race taking a loser back to the barn.

"The piano in the recreation hall doesn't play. It's out of tune. Besides that, we're not particularly liked here. Ever notice that? Nobody ever gives us a fucking tip on a horse, you ever notice that? Nobody tells us a fucking thing!" We were sick of everything, down to the kind of light we had to run horses in. *Loser light,* we called it.

Buddy and Jewel were going down to Ocala, Florida, for a working vacation, and said we could go with them, if we wanted to. We didn't have enough money, but the Fisks were willing to help us if we needed it. It even looked as though there might be some yearlings at the training track for Buddy to break, and he'd need grooms. At least two.

"Are you gonna drink in Florida?" Richard asked.

"Yeah, Richard, I'm going to drink, and you're going to drink right along with me. What's changed?"

We went to Ocala and, as expected, ended up working at the training track—a huge change of pace. I had never been around yearlings before. Their innocence—a quality I'd assumed never left a horse—was of a kind different from the innocence of the horses I'd been with at the track. These horses hadn't been around many people. Their whole bodies articulated awe about the world, and sometimes a colt or a filly would look at me as if startled to be in it.

Sweet Script was looking right through me. Sweet Script was not a very nice filly. She was temperamental and nervous and didn't like to be touched. We didn't think she'd do too well when it came time to stake out a career at the races because she was so flighty and unpredictable.

In some ways, that filly reminded me of myself in terms

of Richard. I, too, had been flighty and unpredictable and not knowing at times what to do with a lover's hand on me. The difference was that Sweet Script was dangerous. One morning when I was walking her around the barn, she suddenly planted herself on a turn and cow-kicked me an inch below my crotch. The black and blue mark lasted two weeks and crawled green into gray from my right hip down to just above the knee. Later that year, Sweet Script dumped the jockey, Jacinto Vasquez, at the starting gate at Gulfstream Park and ran the race without him. She was retired soon after that.

Sweet Script was a harbinger of the lack of talent that was to fill the barn. Even though it was hard to tell conclusively at this stage in their training, evidence suggested that not one horse we had our hands on in Ocala would ever amount to much. If we had been at the races, all our work would have been that much more useless, but because the horses here were yearlings and weren't in serious training yet, our tasks and their tasks were simpler. The early training consisted mainly of galloping once around the track and on most occasions without wraps.

"Leave them open," Buddy or Jewel would instruct us before leaving for the day. From my tenure at the track, I had become so used to bandages on horses that the sight of them now in the stalls with no halters or white cottons wrapped around their legs startled me. *What did they ever need from us? Who were we?*

Off the training track, Richard and I were transients living in the First Lady, a long trailer set down on the farm that belonged to an old friend of Jewel's named Ruthie. She was an ethereal-looking woman we met the day we got to Ocala and never saw again after that. We had no running water in the First Lady, and had to take turns walking to a pump in the stable area where Ruthie boarded horses that were finished at the races or never got there.

Like those horses, Richard and I were finished at the races, too, because this was a Florida away from tourism. There was very little to do aside from working with the yearlings. In the evenings, Richard and I would stop off for a six-pack of beer and sit in the car parked beside the First Lady.

"How long do you think we'll be doing this?" I asked Richard. The sun was descending in a cloudless and fiery sky.

"Well, I'm in it for the long haul."

"Really?" I was surprised. Weren't we going back to New York eventually? "Don't you miss New York?"

"Not at all. But you do, don't you?"

"Yeah, I miss some of it. I don't miss being by myself there. I want to be with you, but I guess I want to see if we can be somewhere else together."

"This is somewhere else."

I nodded slowly.

"You don't want to be with horses, do you?"

And the way the question was phrased, I knew that we would never go back to a life of only us together. Richard came with horses now.

I fell silent for a beat. Then I said softly, "I can't really see myself doing this kind of work forever, unless, of course, another Star of Monaga should come along. Or something better. Don't you want that? Don't you want to have a horse that can run?" I knew he didn't, but it was more important to hear myself say that *I* did.

"It doesn't mean everything to me," Richard said a bit defensively.

"Well, it doesn't mean everything to me either, but it's something to work for. It makes it all seem less repetitious, somehow."

"I'm fine with it. I like who I am with horses. They calm me," he said, proudly.

The relationship Richard had with horses was a much more honest one than I had or would ever have. Since I'd been spoiled by working with Kim Green, horses now interested me only if they had talent—like the people who used to interest me when I was studying acting. In drama students, I was looking for what I had just discovered in myself: something that could set me apart. Was it talent?

"We'll see what happens," I said.

"Look at that sky," Richard said quietly, as if it had turned cold suddenly and he could see his breath in it.

"It's gorgeous, isn't it," I said. The sun was caught in a tree and a line of small birds were arching on the top, pushing on it. The sight of the world at that moment made me homesick for a place I'd never been. "Gorgeous and sad," I said.

"What's sad about it?" Richard said hypnotically.

But all I could do was look over at him in the darkening silence until it was unbearable and I had to put a cassette into the tape player. I didn't know what was sad about the sky or anything else, for that matter, but I wanted to move beyond what had suddenly joined us—silent and huge. I wanted to turn homesickness into a sound. With a backbeat.

We walked into the First Lady with our arms around each other. The light had come on in the stable area, and an old mare had her head under it. I suppose Richard and I were having a domestic life. The car ran, the television worked, the sex was good. We read to each other. We cooked. We took long walks into the woods behind Ruthie's infirmary barn and made love in a bedroom that smelled of lavender candle wax, damp fiberboard, and peppermint tea. We took pictures.

The only two snapshots I have of Richard are without me. In one, he's lying on a bed in powder-blue sneakers with yellow laces drinking a beer and looking at the camera as if he's about to say something untrue. The other photograph is of Richard standing in a barn with a black Labrador named Pepper at his feet. The photos have no particular significance, I realize now. They were not taken during days that held any great meaning or newfound love. Nothing extraordinary was happening and they didn't catch a moment as much as simply repeat one—but they're one of the few things I have left after our twelve years together.

On the last night in Ocala, I had a dream in which Richard and I were separated by a horse. In the dream, I'm working for some trainer in California and I've got my hands on a champion that I'm taking around the country. Richard goes home eventually, back to his father in Ohio, and the horse and I travel around the world—but not in races. In the trees. The dream suddenly turns—we're doing a play about a man and a magical horse who keeps getting the man out of precarious situations by taking him up just before trouble strikes and hiding him in the trees. In the trees, the horse disappears suddenly. The leaves seem to take him. But then the horse appears, like a getaway car, when the man is on level ground and being chased down an alley. Then again, the horse, flying this time—when the man's fallen from a roof. The plot of the dream is sketchy, to say the least—absurdist. And the horse makes anything seem possible. The horse gives the dream its text.

When I woke up I had the same feeling I'd have after a night of flying dreams—as if I'd thrown back a shutter on an alternate world. In flying dreams, the sense I brought with me into waking life was that I could fly anytime I wanted to. I simply chose not to. Like the dream you think is real life, the flying dream always feels ironically more like real life. The other revelation of the horse dream was that Richard's leaving didn't have to be sad. The loss was similar to having to put down an astonishing book once the last page was turned. It felt inevitable. But the dream also suggested that Richard had some part in making the horse do those heroic things. Richard was powerful, too, but I couldn't see it—power implied.

The next day, we were on the road—in real time. We left Buddy and Jewel and Ocala for Hialeah Racetrack that December because Richard was itching to get back to the races. The decision to go to Hialeah was one of the most coherent ones we'd made since hitting the racetrack circuit. Hialeah was the best place to be in winter. All the top outfits from New York were there, so maybe we'd be moving into a new era of horse business where the luck wouldn't be so hard. Even though Richard had said time and time again that it was the work and not any prize afterwards that was golden to him when it came to racehorses, he also began to realize we were broke and figured at least at Hialeah he might cash a bet or two. Betting was something Richard was good at.

We did manage to have enough money for Richard to buy me a Ford Galaxie. Because I've never been able to read the gauges on a dashboard except the one that indicates the tank is empty, the hood blowing open at seventy-five mph mystified me. Richard was furious, briefly. Somehow that sad powder-blue car ditched in a cornfield was a sorry sight but not one worthy of retribution. It was too good an image and we both knew it. We just didn't know what it meant. Luckily for us, there was another car, the trusty Vista Cruiser Richard bought in Ocala. We drove down to Hialeah with high hopes, but these dissolved into despair upon arrival. There was no work and we had to live that first week in the Vista Cruiser parked in the backstretch lot.

Each morning we got our cups of Cuban coffee served in the same paper cups in which hospitals dispense their pills, and like some of those pills, the muddy brew sent us to the stratosphere in about seven seconds. It was the middle of the racing meet and all the outfits were pretty set when it came to hired help. Still, people were quitting and getting fired all the time on the racetrack. We'd seen enough of that back in Ohio to know that we weren't in full doom, here in the sunny middle of little Cuba.

Hialeah is grand. You enter the park through a gate on the

stable side. There are rows of pale yellow and green barns laid out in the same direction, all bordering on a dirt horse trail that is lined for half a mile or so with palm trees. The trail leads into a walking ring and a sudden aviary: a sweet little park in the back of a rose marble grandstand. But the most spectacular sight of birds happens on the day Hialeah runs the Flamingo Stakes for three-year-olds. A dozen or so of the pink namesakes are dramatically let loose on the infield before the start of the race.

The Flamingo Stakes was a race with a sense of ritual I hadn't witnessed before. While watching the birdmen scramble to recapture the flamingos before the horses were off and running (a distraction with untold consequences), I became aware that at this racetrack, people really respected the sport. This was an entirely different view from the one that prevailed at River Downs, Beulah Park, or Latonia. Horses transcended their basic potential for making money and were lifted here into the "something special" category.

What I knew beforehand about Hialeah came from a remake of *The Champ,* the movie starring Jon Voight and Ricky Schroeder, which had been shot here. In it, Hialeah looked like the most elegant racetrack in America—an F. Scott Fitzgerald kind of racetrack. Aside from the palms, the marble, and all the stake races, there was something beautiful about the quality of the afternoons, after the races, when the sun was still shaking in the trees a little and so many of the racetrack denizens were sitting out in the walking rings between barns or on the path under the palms. Everyone was talking about the races and drinking and smoking cigarettes and dope. From that perspective, a day at the races was something sweet and buoyant.

What was so unusual about the clan of horsemen at Hialeah was their utter lack of pretension. For most of my life, dabbling in one art or another, there was always at least a fringe of wannabes and seekers of renown brushstroking my social life with veneer instead of color. What I respected in the horsemen was that their life stories didn't have to be only about themselves: like the beautiful story about Horatio Luro, a trainer who had his top horse, Tap Shoes, down at Hialeah. There was a foal born to a mare that Luro had once trained. One day, while she was turned out in the field with her newborn filly, there was a terrible storm. The mare was struck by lightning and killed. When it came time to name the foal, they called her Lightning Orphan.

After a week or so we finally did manage to get jobs. Richard started working for José Rivera, a New York outfit that was somewhat sloppy and hot-tempered. Whenever I'd come over to visit, the mood on the shedrow was not unlike that of a New York street fair—loud music, singing, and dancing. Everyone seemed to be friends, connected by more than just the outfit.

I had gotten a job hotwalking for John Veitch, who was training for Calumet Farm, and since I hadn't been on the top racing circuit long enough to get a grooming job, I had to go back to the beginning of the race that had started in Cincinnati. But there were better horses this time. Richard hadn't been on the top circuit either, but he knew a lot more about horses than I did and that was enough for Rivera.

Besides that, Richard spoke Spanish—what half the outfit was speaking.

On my first day in the Calumet stable I looked into a padded stall. Before Dawn, the filly who lived there, was a ferocious kicker. She was also the new two-year-old champion and one of the cover fillies on a monthly magazine called *The Blood Horse,* which I had just started reading. The magazine contained wonderful photographs and articles about what was happening to the world I was waking up in every morning, and reading it gave me the insight that life on the racetrack had a wider scope than I had ever imagined. The fact that there was an audience for all of this besides us desperadoes, brokenhearted drunks, and gamblers was a discovery that made the business more viable. The life I'd been led into by Richard was actually known, actually lived. Horses were more than just a metaphor.

But since I was the new kid on the block, horses might as well have been metaphors. It looked as if I wasn't ever going to rub horses for John Veitch—his help had been with him for years, and no one was going anywhere, not with all the races they were winning—so I started working for Rivera as soon as a groom's job became available.

I didn't have great horses to rub. The only one that showed an ounce of talent was Tow Rope, a filly sired by Kentucky Derby winner Riva Ridge. I was looking forward to seeing her run, but on the morning Tow Rope was entered in the sixth race, something devastating happened. Spoils of War, one of the top horses in the stable, came back to the barn after training, stricken and shocked and weaving in the horse ambulance, a pick-up truck with a ramp leading down from the back. When Rivera took the horse down to the path, both horse and trainer were glowing darkly with disaster. Spoils of War's leg was broken at the knee and dangling by a tendon. He was going into shock, eyes wet without tears, hypnotized and terrified at once.

A horse in shock won't eat and eventually dies. More critical, however, was the fact that Spoils's injury was clearly inoperable, so a doctor was called in to administer a lethal injection. After the needle went into the horse's neck, Spoils of War reared up about fifteen feet and let out a wail that sent stable help from all over the racetrack running into the outfit. For many, it was their first experience of a horse dying and a great communal manifestation of grief rose over another realization—that for every celebration of a stake win or cashing in of tickets on a speedball at 10 to 1, there was a horse that suffered like Spoils of War.

Watching the horse crumble in the ring of smoke he made by stomping out his last message in the cracked brown earth made me think of a horse I saw go down, but easier, at Belmont Park, where I'd gone with my stepfather so many years ago. I'd bet on a long shot that day, and the horse I'd wagered on fell at the top of the stretch, turning for home.

"Oh my God," I said and turned to my stepfather, not believing what I was seeing. "What happened?"

"That's what you get for betting on a long shot. The horse was probably hurting going into the race."

"And they made him run anyway?"

"Yeah . . . well . . . trainers are a betting bunch."

Driving back to Brooklyn, still reeling from the sight of the fallen horse, I was lost in a cloud until my stepfather asked me, "What do you think?"

"I think racehorses are sad."

"Well, they don't all break down, you know. That was beginner's bad luck."

"Why do you bet money on them?"

"Because I can win.

"But you never know when you'll win."

"Exactly—that's what keeps it exciting."

"They're sad," I said again.

But I didn't actually think racehorses were sad, not really. I said that, it occurs to me now, to take some of my stepfather's sadness away from him by putting it inside the very game that fed his addiction. I should have said, "I think *you're* sad," but we didn't have a relationship with a window in it to let direct sunlight through.

"When do you win?" I asked my stepfather in the final collapse of day across the Brooklyn sky when all that was left became a peach-colored reflection wiped across the windshield of a Vista Cruiser that should have been sold for parts.

When do you win? And he kept on driving.

In 1990, my stepfather died of a heart attack while waiting for dinner in the mental ward of Downstate Hospital in Brooklyn, the same hospital he checked into after my mother died. I hadn't spoken to my stepfather for nearly a decade. Rage and indifference had mixed with clouds of memory. I'd heard from my brother that, a couple of years after our mother's death, my stepfather had started living with a woman who was barely functional and had gone from being someone extremely fastidious to something of a sloven. When I heard about his death, all I was able to call to mind was a frightening photograph that had appeared in the *Daily News* just months before. While being transferred from one hospital to another, my stepfather had taken a pair of scissors and had used them to threaten the driver of the ambulance. It was a picture of someone I literally didn't recognize, until a friend pointed out to me that the caption under the grainy shot identified a man who had the same name as mine.

I had been legally adopted by my stepfather as soon as he married my mother. After my natural father divorced my mother, he married again and disappeared into Germany. Supposedly he'd gone there for business reasons, but he had also just thrown a man who was fucking a girlfriend out a second-story window.

I lived with my natural father at various early stages of my life, when my mother was hospitalized for long durations in psychiatric wards in New Haven or New York, but I never felt strongly about him because I never really knew him. He was tall and blond, a Yale graduate, an Air Force pilot. And always a figure to me—a figure, not a whole person, because I never heard him admit he was wrong, or saw him naked, or ever heard him cry. But he was good to me after my mother died. I called him in Germany and he sent me a ticket to come visit him in Dusseldorf, where he lived on the Rhine.

If you can blame a person for someone's death—outside of murder—I blamed my stepfather for my mother's. In part, anyway. In the wake of my grief, I just kept thinking she would still be alive if she'd never met him. My stepfather and I hadn't been able to reconcile anything between us, including the sex. He died after having taken the trouble to state what he couldn't give me as a codicil in his will: *And to my stepson, Michael Klein, I leave nothing.* But he did leave me something. He left me the spoils of war.

The Rivera barn circled around the Rivera horse, motionless now on the sparse grass, his body flattened. You could hear the horse's breathing slowly coming to an end as he tried to roll over once but fell back to his original position and finally died. Rivera was crying, but the vet just stood there for a while with an expression on his face that was hard to gauge—somewhere between guilt and indifference, certainly not anything like sadness. It made me angry—his standing there over death, with a face like that.

We moved back slowly to the work we had left before the horse went down. I walked into the stall of the horse I was finishing up and looked for a long time into one of his big eyes that reflected the shock settling into sadness in my face. But I was sad for other reasons, too. Richard had decided to stay at Hialeah while I went with the Rivera outfit to New York. I would be leaving him in two days.

Buddy and Jewel had gotten their stalls here, and for some reason I simply couldn't fathom, Richard had decided to leave Rivera to work for the Fisks again. It was such a strange dance backward and against everything we had talked about, specifically that we would work only for New York outfits as long as we were both going to be committed to the business. I thought that Richard's decision didn't indicate any real allegiance to the Fisks but was forced by his not wanting to go where I was headed—back to New York again. There were too many bad memories there for both of us, and Richard felt them more deeply than I did.

Worst of all, I couldn't imagine being in the horse business without Richard there beside me, or even being in New York without him. He had led me into this labyrinth, after all, and any success I'd achieved—which was then limited to making the transition to a better set of horses—was due in large part to Richard's physical and mentorial presence. We never discussed his decision to stay at Hialeah. While I stood there in the stall with a living horse on the edge of Spoils's death, a remnant from my subconscious surfaced. Part of my dream that last night in Ocala was coming true. Richard was disappearing. But where was the horse?

Lost in a meadow on Claiborne Farm. John Sosby, the farm manager, couldn't find the yearling anywhere that morning until he heard the sound of snoring from the low-lying part of the pasture. Because the original name of Foghorn had already been registered with the Jockey Club of America, Claiborne decided to honor the place where they found their horse one lazy afternoon, when the world was just a field to eat. The yearling would be called Swale.

And Swale was coming closer.

Nine

Dead Dogs and Thrown Riders

I grew up in a world of landscapes in motion. I remember when my mother took me to see the Amazing Randi, the famous illusionist, I was struck most not by the departure or the mechanics of how something disappeared but that the thing—the scarf, the bird, the globe—could actually come back, that the space between the thing here and the thing gone wasn't total, but as transitory as the word *abracadabra!*

Before I was a teenager, we moved at least a dozen times—

to Alexandria, Virginia, various towns in Connecticut, and then to New York where we lived on West Twelfth Street. After a year, we moved up the block, then to Central Park West, and finally to three places in Brooklyn before I ventured out on my own. Without roots, the temporal shine on everything meant a kind of freedom, but it was also a curse. My childhood rode on top of vanishing. What was there one minute was often gone the next. That anyone could actually have a connection to land astonished me. What grounded me was sensory, something in the air I breathed, not the gravitational earth.

Along with grief and the spirit of reconciliation, the other thing I brought with me to River Downs was a fascination for illusion. Riding the van full of Rivera's horses going to New York, I realized that all my *Blood Horse* reading had begun to make text and images out of that illusion, and I started following the careers of certain horses and trainers.

The one name that leapt off the page was the trainer Woody Stephens. I'd noticed him first at Hialeah. Stephens always had some remarkable first-time starter or was winning a stake race every couple of weeks, and from all the reports in *The Blood Horse,* he was clearly the leading trainer in New York. Woody Stephens was stabled in the exclusive section of Belmont Park called Millionaire's Row, the yellow brick road of barns turned over season after season to the trainers who had the horses winning the most races.

As I was watching Rivera's horses taking nervous bites out of the hayracks that hung beside their heads like dismantled wreaths, I thought a job with Stephens would be the pinnacle of working at Belmont Park—an arsenal of horsepower I hadn't known firsthand at Hialeah. Pulling into New York was intimidating and utterly different from returning to a place I'd ever lived. It didn't seem to register that I'd drank so much as a cup of coffee on a street in Hell's Kitchen, so I couldn't imagine going back to the old neighborhood, even on a day off.

The ride from Florida to New York was undramatic except when the van pulled in at a truck stop along the way. Then, more than our getting a view of the outside world, the outside world got a view of us, and no matter how many times they'd been used to what must have been a hundred vans a year, the truckers and waitresses were always surprised to see all of us tumbling out of them, straw in our creases, bleary-eyed—what horses did to us. Nobody expects horses, especially racehorses. They belong in a barn or on a television or in the movies when they're not a blur across their speed course, a bit hidden from civilization. The racetrack itself, I had learned over the years, was a mirage to most people.

It was a long and sleepy ride in the van. And claustrophobic. Horses took up most of the room and the members of the outfit camped out anywhere there was enough space at a safe distance from the animals. The country sped blindly by while I slept or muttered to horses about nothing in particular. And it was a lonelier ride because of the two languages in the van. While some of the attempts at English by the crew were admirable, any attempt of mine at Spanish was unintelligible. I stammered along and smoked cigarettes far away enough from the hayracks so they wouldn't catch on fire. I was thinking about what it would be like to have sex in a horse van.

And about Richard. I was afraid of being alone in the new version of this. Whom would I possibly befriend? I had become painfully aware of the fact that on the track I had never really tried to extend myself to other people, except sexually. With Richard gone, it felt as if I would simply have to fall deeper into my work with the horses to fill the void he left. Did I want to fall deeper?

Strangely enough, I rarely entertained the notion of actually getting off the racetrack. I'm not sure why that was, except that I was broke and had no one in New York to call on for any kind of support. Richard and I had done a thorough job of keeping most people at bay. I suppose the consistency of having a job and a paycheck every week was important. Because I had been such a loose horse myself so many times, through evictions, drunken escapades, and sexual whirling, I suppose I also needed the structure that a life with horses gave me. The work kept me strangely focused, like the man with the horse in my dream. I had to pay attention, no matter how much I drank. But how much I drank was also keeping me from knowing any other option.

By the time we landed in New York, the fear I had brought with me about how I'd make it without Richard had all but disappeared. There was something about the look of Belmont Park that captivated me immediately. It was springtime and everything was green except the blossoms on the cherry trees that lined the first row of barns beyond the main gate. The barns were green and long and rose alongside winding horse paths that led to the track, which seemed in that first, uneducated look to be miles away. Famous races for famous horses happened there. And every year there was the running of the Belmont Stakes, the third jewel in the Triple Crown and the longest race in the series. Richard said any horse that made it to the third jewel was already a champion.

Tack rooms like the ones I had been accustomed to living in at River Downs and Hialeah were now replaced by little buildings further away from the barns. The only drawback was that because the number of rooms was calculated by the number of horses in the stable (and we seemed to have more help than we needed), I had to share with three guys a room that was the size of two knocked-over telephone booths.

The most beautiful horse in the stable was its star, Christmas Past, a filly that had made a remarkable showing down in Florida and had the look and temperament of a champion: she was a bitch. Everything else in the barn paled next to the statuesque, dappled-gray prize filly, and any prestige that came from working in Rivera's barn was from the association we all had, at least indirectly, with her. There wasn't a horse in any other stall that had nearly the ability Christmas Past had. She was keeping us in business, and we all knew it.

In the first few weeks of settling in, getting to know a few people and starting to rub new horses Rivera had gotten from Kentucky and Argentina, the beauty of Belmont was enough to hold me. But working for Rivera became unsatisfying. I hadn't been with him long enough to be considered for grooming any of the few good horses. No one in the outfit ever did like me. And nothing I was rubbing would amount to much. I was in charge of one thoroughbred that was so huge, no amount of training could make him fit—at least in my beginner's estimation. His name was Hab Dancer. I called him Fat Dancer. Rivera could never get him fit enough to run, so he shipped him off to England where, unbelievably, a year later he ended up breaking the track record.

I was also given a gray two-year-old by Gray Dawn II (Christmas Past's sire) called Nico's Hope that was the meanest horse I'd ever touched. I was actually afraid to go into his stall, and each morning I'd have to enact a routine so he'd let me keep my life. I knew never to sneak up on a horse like this or to enter his stall while his back was to me. I would coax him up to the front—simply by calling his name—and run to the back of the stall with a chain that I would then hook to his halter as soon as he turned around. This safety procedure worked most of the time.

Then, one morning, as I was cleaning out his back hoof, Nico kicked my hand so hard that he broke my right index finger. I was out of work for a week. For some strange and unsettling reason, the time off suddenly made me the object of desire for a few of the boozers under Rivera's shedrow. It seemed that whenever they got enough liquor in them, these guys would go after the "queer." Liquor camels, I called them—they seemed drunk whether they'd been drinking or not.

These guys were pretty insistent about getting me to fuck with them and rather than go to Rivera himself to complain— it would have gotten me nowhere since Rivera wasn't too crazy about me to begin with—I locked myself in my room. I don't know what made me so puritanical, actually. There had certainly been enough times in my life when I would have fucked anything that moved. What was different now? Perhaps physical pain had given me a little more self-respect.

In the week I was out of work, Nico's Hope broke his back leg in an ordinary gallop once around the track and had to be destroyed. Supernatural, I remember thinking. And it marked the beginning of what seemed like a six-month reel of omens—strange scenes that got played out through the weeks in the once tranquil setting of Belmont Park:

Dead dogs and thrown riders.

Sidewinder, the senile German shepherd with a crooked spine that Woody Stephens owned, dead and buried one afternoon under a driftwood cross.

Horses coming out of near-fatal fevers and going on to win stake races.

A vet in the barn in the middle of the night with a flashlight and a notebook.

Horse testicles baking on a roof, thrown there right after castration, for luck.

Too Chic, the trainer Jim Maloney's important filly, casually trotting down Hempstead Turnpike.

A long black Cadillac parked in a paddock, its motor running and in the back seat the singer Carole Bayer Sager, who owned a horse named Heartlight.

Screen doors blown off in windstorms.

Dirty dishes in a field.

My body falling out of a horse van and onto a metal horse-path sign, which made a two-inch gash below my heart.

My naked body falling down a flight of twenty stairs—drugged.

My drunk body asleep in the corner of a horse's stall. Rivera calmly asked me the next morning what I was doing there.

"I just stumbled in, I guess. I was drunk."

"You're fired," came the reply.

This was the culminating blow in a particularly grisly, drunken weekend. Two days before I had met and became friendly with an Argentinian maniac called Flacko, who was an assistant trainer—at least that's what everyone said. It was hard to believe. The man Flacko worked for had some of the best horses on the grounds, and I couldn't see a boss turning any of their training over to someone who seemed even half as flaky as Flacko was. But I found Flacko attractive, figured he was gay, and jumped at an invitation one night to go to his room, which was in a building that looked like a low-rise apartment house—a startling sight on the racetrack, even if it was Belmont Park.

After drinking a bottle of vodka and getting into a pillow fight with Flacko and three of his exercise-boy pals, he suddenly got very serious, grabbed my arm, and dragged me to the window.

"What the fuck are you doing?" I screamed, genuinely terrified and shocked sober. Flacko held me out the window for about three minutes and finally pulled me in, laughing with the other exercise boys as if he had succeeded at something he didn't know he was good at. The whole scene reminded me of a sad story about my mother when she was in boarding school and how her classmates had hung her by the heels out the window one morning—the final strike in a series of blows all around the fact that she was overweight.

As bad as the scene was, I was still attracted to Flacko. When he invited me the next week to a trainer's apartment in town he was housesitting for, Flacko greeted me at the door with a butcher knife, which he quickly and very deliberately held against my quivering throat.

"C'mon, Flacko, stop it."

He pulled the knife away, but it wasn't warning enough. I still walked into the apartment as if I had taken Flacko's threat as a come-on. I'd known the guy a week, he'd tried to murder me twice, and I wanted him. The tone of this particular scene wasn't any more dissonant than the music I thought I could hear during those desperate forays to the Anvil, accompanying me and my zombie walk across the dance floor—a case of beer already in me—ready to meet my murderer. I never got hurt in that after-hours palace, but I was certainly looking to get hurt by Flacko, who, as soon as my back was turned, lit the shirt I was wearing on fire. The flame burned through the scary script of the show the T-shirt was advertising: *Sweeney Todd, the Demon Barber of Fleet Street.*

Flacko's insane behavior wasn't a private performance I had willingly taken a seat in the theater to watch. He was crazy in public, too, and was picked up by the police three weeks later after he jumped out of the bushes somewhere near the track, grabbed a woman, and raped her.

Being out of work on the track was a very scary thing because this was the only place I *could* work—too far from other kinds of jobs and the city. Without a job, I was cut loose from the mother ship and was floating in space. Free time was a luxury so foreign to me now that I didn't know what to do with it except sleep and drink.

In the floating week, I staggered from drink to drink and took long breaks under huge trees that darkened the world. Greentree Stable's barn, one of the best outfits at Belmont, was the first stable inside the gate on Elmont Road. The trees and what I could see through them gave me a different perspective on Belmont Park than the one I had while working with Rivera. The track seemed like a quieter place. I got to talk to people as they streamed by on horseback or on foot—on a break from the barn when they would run across to O'Brien's bar for a quick shot of schnapps or a beer. I met a pony girl one morning who worked for Woody Stephens. They were looking for a groom, and I stumbled over and was hired on barely a recommendation. I didn't even mention Rivera. The only thing Billy Carter, Stephen's foreman, knew was what he could see by looking at me. I was strong.

I was hired to work in the two-year-old barn whose help went to Aiken, South Carolina, each winter to break babies. Woody had two barns at Belmont: one for the babies, working toward their first race, and another barn full of stake horses. He also had two houses for the help: one for whites and one for blacks. Everybody knew about it, accepted it, and didn't dare call it racist. Still, I was astonished. The arrangement gave me the creepy feeling I had when Commissioner Gabe lay on top of the manure pile and the racetrack froze in time. Something was terribly wrong.

Anyway, I was ecstatic to be working for Stephens, and

when Billy Carter said he was looking for another groom, I called Richard, in Florida, to tell him. Richard and I hadn't talked since I'd gotten to New York. What would I have told him—that I'd been fired by Rivera? Now I had better news and more than just a tip about a job. When I called down to Florida, Jewel said that Richard had left them a couple of weeks before to go home to Ohio where his mother was recovering from open-heart surgery. The news of the surgery reminded me that Richard's whole family had never been strangers to health problems or even more startling tragedy. His father's second wife was found murdered in the kitchen one afternoon, but more important, to me anyway, was Richard's attempted suicide, long before I met him. His father discovered him in 1966, hanging from a rope in a college dorm: near death from a crushed lung and a broken heart (the boy didn't love him back) that gave him the nerve to stand on the chair in the first place.

I realized during the phone call that I missed Richard, which felt sudden rather than cumulative, as though the sound of his voice substantiated a longing I'd forgotten I had—a longing, I suppose too, for re-identification. When Richard managed to get to New York a week later, Billy Carter put him to work right away. And liked him right away, too.

Richard told me that Woody Stephens was the best trainer on the East Coast—famous for getting dazzling speed out of horses. Stephens also had panache and an uncanny way of getting press attention—whenever the outfit took a first-time starter over to the races, all eyes were on us. Stephens always had the horse to beat, and it put a euphoria in the barn enough times for it to become rhythmic. It was all like a dream, now. Through a series of sidetrips, Richard and I had finally landed in the same powerful shedrow. We'd arrived.

Woody Stephens had done everything on the racetrack. His stature as a leading trainer came after a long life of getting up before dawn and working in the barns in Kentucky, which was where he was from. In the early 1900s, those hills outside his hometown of Midway were fast becoming the center of the thoroughbred world. Stephens started out as a jockey—a bad one, so the story goes. He was slight in build but won only a couple of times. When the riding gig wasn't giving Woody the career he'd envisioned, his trainer fostered Woody's potential as an astute conditioner and finally gave him some horses to train. Eventually, after those horses won some important races, Woody got the reputation as someone who could get a horse to the front end and make him stay there.

Then he connected with some millionaires who supplied him year after year with the best yearlings they could breed or buy. When I went to work for him, ninety percent of the horses trained by Woody Stephens were winning stakes every other week.

I held Stephens in an awe that was deepened by the fact that I rarely saw him. He'd come over to the baby barn only when he had to—usually just before he left for the day—to reassure himself that the horses were all right. I quickly learned that being in Barn Four, as I was, meant being tied to drugs— alcohol, heroin. Some of the crew in the baby barn were addicts. By sending the grooms in Barn Four to Aiken, Woody was not providing vacation time or trusting anyone outside the range of his watchful eye—as it might have appeared to an outsider. He was simply removing the personnel in Barn Four from the New York premises for the winter—to get their act together.

Billy Carter warned me that if I were ever to get my hands on a horse down south that showed an ounce of potential as a runner, it would quickly be snatched away and walked over to the main barn when we returned to Belmont Park in the spring. I took this as a challenge to myself. If I got a good one down in Aiken, I'd do anything to keep him. I was working for Woody Stephens now, and I wanted it to stay that way.

While there were grooms in Barn Four who had been with Stephens for a while, the mainstay of grooms were in Barn Three, the stake barn, and they'd been with him even longer. Why would anyone quit? This was a crew that almost unanimously idolized Stephens and did anything that was asked of them. It was also a group that consisted largely of African American men in their forties and fifties. And characters, all.

Ben Dove spoke with a drawl and a lisp, and drank beer as soon as he got done with his morning work. Ben was also from Kentucky and had been with Woody longer than anybody else. When he had a couple of beers in him, Ben would bask in Stephens's sunlight and talk about the dozen or so times he'd visited the winner's circle. If a racehorse down in Aiken was going to move into Barn Three, it usually moved into one of Dove's stalls. Over the years, Ben had sat under the cream of Woody's crop: De La Rose, White Star Line, Bemissed, What's Dat, Sabin—all champions that made Dove a great deal in stake money.

I respected Dove but didn't like him much. He seemed unusually bitter for someone who'd been so lucky. And possessive. Dove expected the best horses. All he had to do was wait. Those stake horses that seemed to drop out of the sky didn't really mean Woody considered Dove to be his best worker. The fact was, Ben yessed Stephens more than anyone else on the shedrow. And, as it turned out, he snitched to Woody about the help. But what could Ben have disclosed? The help was getting high or drunk, but Woody was fully aware of that.

There was no one working for Woody Stephens whose drinking problem concerned him more than his own brother, Bill. Bill was my boss, along with Billy Carter, and he was strict, funny, and much more talkative than Woody. Booze-talkative. Bill Stephens had allies in grooms David Major, Bennie Breeze, Chip Sinclair, and me. The sight of him coming back to the barn every afternoon for evening feeding and smuggling in a bottle of vodka wrapped in a loose page out of the *Daily Racing Form* always amused us. From whom was Bill hiding? We were all drunk so much of the time; we were his brothers in dissolution, for God's sake. We kept him company.

Bill was the saddest kind of alcoholic—deadened but not dead. I don't think I ever saw him completely sober. Apparently, the years before Belmont Park had been different for Bill. Some people around Belmont who knew Bill from Kentucky said he was a better horseman than Woody and that booze had killed his talent. We'd never know what he was or could have been. One morning in 1983, Bill's wife found him dead from a heart attack. I was washing mud and grass stains out of horse bandages in Aiken, South Carolina, when I heard the news from a shocked Billy Carter.

For weeks afterward, I thought of Bill Stephens, alive in the crumbling Chevrolet he so often parked at the training track. The car's front door was thrown open so Bill could call out to a horse over the music from the radio. He was always loose and illogical, throwing back beers and letting himself get wrapped in the scattered pages of a newspaper. But after Richard, it was probably Bill Stephens who taught me the most about grooming a racehorse, and I listened to him carefully. He was funny, he loved the sport, and he was a drunk, which made him an instant peer, no matter what his station in life may have been. And so, when Bill showed me how to walk into a stall (slowly), talk to a horse (softly), and hide a bottle of booze in the bran barrel (deeply), I didn't have the heart to tell him that I already knew.

Ten

Teachers

I am working for the best outfit in the world.
Woody, my teacher.
Aiken is coming. Fresh horses.
Bill, my teacher.
Richard is in the dark and he will talk in his sleep tonight.
Richard, my teacher.

Eleven

Aiken Breezes

The main street in Aiken, South Carolina, is constantly being interrupted by the live oaks. The interruption gives the town its visual pull because the trees are literally sweeping the streets. But Aiken isn't known for its live oaks or for its moonshine served in baby-food jars that you knocked on a certain door in Laundrytown to get. Or for Highland Park. Aiken is known for young racehorses in serious training for the first time.

Woody Stephens had been coming down here for years. Many of the giants he trained first set foot on the racing strip sequestered here in this hamlet, far away from the betting public and media hounds. Aiken meant being away from the track, which meant that the only money you could make was what you were paid: not much, about $150 per week. For a lot of the help, most of the money went towards getting high. Bennie Breeze and Billy Carter loved coming down to Aiken every year because they could get high a lot more often than they ever could at Belmont Park, with Woody around.

Billy Carter was high in the van going down to Aiken, and we had sex—a shadowy, incomplete kind of sex, jittery and somewhat unbidden. Billy made a drunken pass while we were both lying at the horses' feet and I was too tired to protest. Richard was in the other van. It was 3:00 in the morning and we still had an hour to go before we reached the training track. As vague as that sex was, I thought it might put a good horse in one of my stalls. "You'll get a good horse, Klein," Billy said in his sleep just afterward. "Don't worry, I'll take care of you."

But what difference did it make? Any good horse would be lost to me back in New York. Besides, these were yearlings, just shy of turning two. Buddy Fisk used to say, "You can't tell a good horse until you put a saddle on him." These horses hadn't yet seen a saddle, much less another horse running up to them in the middle of a furlong. They hadn't seen anything in the world except their mothers and stable hands and straw and hay and grass and the round metal bottom of a feed tub that held the only reflection they would ever know: their own indistinct eyes, looking for more.

Bennie Breeze was good around a yearling—better than he was around himself. Like Bill Stephens, Bennie was a sad addict to watch and would disappear every morning for an hour or so and come back a different person—singing a little maniacally and moving so slowly it was hard to believe he could get through the morning in an upright position. Bennie had a particularly rough filly called Reveal, and I always worried about him and the filly whenever he was in the stall and high. As good as Bennie was around horses, Reveal still could have struck and Bennie wouldn't have even known what hit him.

One morning Reveal threw an exercise boy and ran off past the live oaks, the other barns, and onto South Boundary Road, where she stopped in her tracks at the sight of Bennie dressed in a dilapidated brown felt hat with a shank in his hand to lead her back to the barn with. In the other hand, Bennie held a burning cigarette which was down to its last drag. It was a wonderful, slapstick picture. And timeless, too: Bennie's last mission on earth. He died after putting Reveal back in her stall, died with a pitchfork in one hand and twenty hits of black-beauty speed in the other. But his death didn't surprise anyone, which made it that much more tragic. It was a death that had been coming for a long time (heroin, daily).

We all just went home that morning. Everyone was too sad to finish work. Richard picked some wildflowers and laid them in front of Reveal's stall and we drove to Whiskey Road where we had the best accommodations we'd ever had since hitting the racetrack: three rooms—bedroom, living room, and an eat-in kitchen—which felt like a paradise after that morning of death. The most we could manage was to watch *All My Children,* the venerable television soap opera, which we eventually got addicted to.

In a strange way, Bennie's death was a bridge to social life. Like the night Richard and I had counterpointed my mother's death with a transcendent kind of sex because we had felt so mortal, we were now using Bennie's death as a way of reaching out to the world around us. Within a couple of weeks, we'd made a couple of friends who had nothing to do with horses—townspeople—which came as a surprise since Richard and I thought we'd long ago lost whatever used to make us interesting to anyone off the track. Nick Reston was a tennis coach, and Nancy Lewis, who was Nick's friend, was the town's greatest caterer. Nancy loved horses and used to come to the barn just to look at them. She'd even get on a couple of horses sometimes, but not too often. One day she brought Nick and we hit it off instantly.

I quickly realized that there was something about Nick Reston that thrilled me. Richard saw my interest and stole away whenever Nick was around. Nick was straight, but we had crushes on each other—deep, look-at-each-other-for-no-reason-other-than-to-see-how-the-other-recovered-from-the-look crushes. This was the first crush on a straight man I'd ever had—not that it particularly confused me, it had just never happened.

For reasons that neither of us fully comprehended or acknowledged, we sought out each other every day. As the sun was setting, I'd usually be sitting on the front steps of the house, gazing down Whiskey Road as if I were listening to music. Nick would pull up in his red Toyota truck and cut the engine.

"Wanna beer?" Nick smiled.

"Was World War Two noisy?" I aimed back. "Sure I do."
I wasn't going to tell him I was an alcoholic, I'd decided—a
thought that in its forming truly baffled me. I'd go inside and
grab two Tuborgs and set them on the stoop. Richard would
be sleeping or reading. Nick never left his truck. I'd walk his
beer over to him, looking at him the whole time. We'd sit at
either end of the golden distance between us, laughing and
drinking while the sun diffused into its foretold amber. And it
struck me suddenly that this moment was what had been
Ocala's moment in the car and Nick had, in a strange way,
replaced the Richard who drank beers looking at the sad and
gorgeous sky.

I told Nick about my glamorous past in the big city, and
he told me about all the women he'd scored being the humpy
tennis coach in town. Nancy Lewis had been an old love, but
the affair had died out long ago.

"Take me for a ride," I announced. The wish was based
on a longing for music. I had just picked up an Al Jarreau
tape and there was a song on it I wanted Nick to hear. It was
a form of flirtation for me—getting a man to listen to a
song.

The song was an extraordinary ballad called "Not Like
This," about an affair that was over. When it came up on the
tape, I made Nick pull over and listen to it, and in the song's
duration we sat transfixed in a space that was filling up with
an almost operatic longing.

"Isn't that fucking gorgeous," I said.

"Yeah, it is. Yeah," Nick whispered. We sat in the silence

of it, and a minute longer, until the song became a bond between us.

Richard was thoroughly aware of what was happening between Nick and me, but we never talked about it. Still, it was what the growing silence was made of—present while *All My Children* was on; present in the car in the morning drive to work. Perhaps it was a previously undetectable resentment towards Richard, which had begun in Florida, that was moving us closer to the edge of a fault line. Some mercurial piece of that separation was still very much inside of me, and I really hadn't dealt with the anger I might have felt towards Richard until Nick presented himself. It's odd sometimes how the appearance of a stranger in your life can reveal a part of your story that would have never gotten written.

Nothing was going to happen between Nick and me. I knew that. And I suppose, for me, he represented the first really articulate person I had met in a long time. With Nick's arrival, everything I'd truly missed in other people outside the racing world had reappeared, and the exciting, irreversible pull Nick and I had towards each other meant that there was the possibility of not needing Richard in order to substantiate what it was about me that was at all desirable. Richard's old standby love suddenly didn't engage me anymore in Aiken, South Carolina. We were both changing into people who were thinking about what they would remember about each other.

And we kept our silence, which was worsened by the inability to move it anywhere that would take away its emphasis. There was a movie theater up the road, for instance, but we never went to movies. I don't know why that was. It may have been that culture lighting up the dark was threatening or sad to both of us. We had, after all, disappeared from culture.

We had this life and still each other because it was another life.

Twelve

Swale

One rose and blue morning, when the mist was starting to lift from the tops of barns like clouds from the moon and Billy Carter and I were getting through the first few hours without a drink—*Just to see what it's like,* Billy used to say—I was led to a grand-looking black colt that was too big for the stall.

"Klein, take care of this son of a bitch," he said. "He's a good one. He's by the Slew." It was one of the last things Billy Carter ever said to me. A week later, he started bleeding from every orifice and had to be rushed to the hospital. It was the strangest thing I'd ever seen happen to anybody. You had to wear a surgical mask when you went to visit him. All anyone could say was that his blood cells were out of whack—he didn't have enough platelets—and that he couldn't breathe. What the doctors knew in that southern town of old money on one hand, and moonshine in Laundrytown on the other, was that Billy Carter was a black man dying of some strange disease. Nobody paid it much mind. That summer, after a spring of oxygen and days in bed, Billy Carter died of what was about to be called AIDS.

When Billy was in the hospital, I started reading a book about Seattle Slew. There were a lot of photographs of Saratoga Racetrack which made me want to go there, but the most impressive thing was the fact that the Slew had been undefeated as a two-year-old. Woody's specialty was two-year-olds, so I began to imagine the horse Billy Carter gave me to rub might amount to something. And the colt was royally bred. Seattle Slew was the Triple Crown winner of 1977. Tuerta, the colt's mother, was a pretty good grass mare that had won some stakes in New York. The fascinating thing about her was that she was born without a left eye or even a place for one. That side of her face was perfectly smooth.

Each morning when I put the saddle on Swale (I also called him Rudy, after Nureyev) and handed him over to Billy Badgett (Woody's assistant trainer) to get on, I could feel the horse getting stronger. He wasn't the same kind of playful most colts were at that age. Already he was all business, which meant he loved going to the track.

Because good help was scarce in Aiken, especially exercise help, Billy got on Swale himself and took him to the track, galloped him and breezed him his first three-eighths of a mile. Badgett knew immediately about how much pure horse he was sitting on, but he was unsure about Swale's confirmation. The horse was over at the knees, which could mean trouble down the road—too much stress might be taken in the knee area when the horse ran. And knees, like ankles, are very tricky on a racehorse. You can't plan on keeping them sound as long as you're running them. The only thing to do was hope Swale would somehow learn to distribute the stress.

Swale's natural ability impressed Badgett and everyone standing at the outside rail of the training track that winter in Aiken—his way of handling the surface, of looking straight ahead, and of course, his speed. He was a professional and he wasn't even two. Though it's hard to tell how fast a horse will be until he's in company and the competition allows the athlete in him to press down on the accelerator, you can tell early how fast a horse might go. He simply makes the rider on top of him feel as though everything he does takes no effort and that it's painless.

It was love at first sight—or before it—for me. I had the strange feeling that I had loved Swale before ever setting eyes on him and every time I passed his stall it was as though I was looking not so much at a horse but at a place, which made the gaze familiar. Because he was a place I loved, I didn't think Swale would ever hurt me, but I didn't know for sure. He was young, and I had to be especially careful when I went back in the afternoon for feeding not to be too drunk. Aside from the fact that I knew Swale hated drunkenness—he simply ignored me, or shook his head like the humanized horse in the movies that talks or has a sense of humor—I could have been seriously hurt.

One afternoon, as I was placing his feed tub in the stall, Swale sneaked up behind me and grabbed my left ear with his teeth. To this day, I'm amazed he didn't simply bear down and take it. We both just stood there for a minute. I very calmly took my hand and forced his mouth open so he could release me from his grip. Then he did the little dance he always danced when he was feeling good—a jump in the air on his front legs, and two or three head tosses accompanied by snorting, which always sounded like a good laugh to me. Sometimes he'd roll on his back across the whole width of the stall, get up, straw in his mane or foretop, and shake everything off.

From the very beginning I paid an inordinate amount of attention to Swale. He was clearly the best horse I had ever laid a hand on, and if I took care of him, he'd take care of me—emotionally, I hoped, and monetarily. Before Swale, the racetrack existed only in present time—but now there was a future. And Swale was able to get out of me a kind of love that hadn't burned out from drinking. When was the last time I loved anything without thinking too much—without being its judge?

One morning in Aiken's track kitchen I took a dinner knife and carved SWALE = KY. DERBY on the edge of one of the tables as a way of seeing all the good news I was hearing—a trick with a knife to evoke renown. I wasn't objective like Billy

Badgett was. I knew I was in charge of a live one—at least that. There was fire under all that blackness. I also knew that Swale trained in such a way that he avoided injury, and he never exerted more energy than he had to. In his first trial race, he had won by just enough of a margin to put him over the wire first. It was a smart way to go.

Two weeks later, Swale and I got on the van to go back to New York. It was, as usual, a production. Loading twenty or so head of two-year-olds was always trying. They'd only done this walk once, during a break on a Kentucky horse farm—up a slanted board into a metal and hay-smelling darkness. That last day in Aiken, they were all frisky. Swale nuzzled his head into my chest—because he was cold, I suppose, but it was a move that always made me think he was looking for my heart.

I left Aiken in 1982 with only one worry. All this time while we were breaking yearlings and Billy Carter was dying and Bennie Breeze was dead (in the world) and kept dying (in our heads); and Nick Reston and I didn't say goodbye; and I was loving Swale in all his appearing and Richard in his disappearing, there was a doppelgänger two stalls down, a dark horse. I hadn't paid much attention to the bay colt by Herbager, but by the time we left Aiken for Belmont Park, I knew this horse was going to get all the attention. People were talking about him the way they talked about Swale. I could feel the future like a chill across my heart until even the doppelgänger's name scared me. The horse's name was Devil's Bag.

Thirteen

Swale's Heart

Two clear facts were keeping me awake in the van riding out of the South: Swale was special, and I was moving further and further away from Richard. I couldn't explain to Richard how Nick Reston defined desire or how my love for Swale opened up a life I was more interested in, but something had changed. I couldn't go back to what I had with Richard before Aiken or Swale, not because there was no love there but because the force of Swale felt progressive to me, and the idea of Richard had started to feel regressive.

On the other hand, I was still drinking, and as lovely a metaphor as Swale was becoming, he was also providing an escape. I didn't have to work on the relationship with Swale the way I had to work on the one with Richard. I was unable to allow the patience, understanding, or even the love for another person to take hold.

When we got to New York, Woody wanted to run Swale and break his maiden as soon as possible. The trainer hadn't seen the colt train down south, and he wanted to see firsthand what he was made of. Woody had already heard that Swale was something special, so I think his heart was probably in the same place mine had been in when I carved the horse's magic formula into a table in Aiken. But Woody didn't believe in little rituals. The trainer was a businessman and he thrived on solid proof.

My horse had certainly come to New York with enough pre-publicity, but it was nothing like the attention given to Devil's Bag, who was already Woody's number one two-year-old. The Bag was a faster horse than Swale, but his speed caused a lot of us in the barn to feel that he just wouldn't last as long. It was a speed that was reckless, unmethodical, and wild—a mustang's speed. Devil's Bag was headed toward the first tier of two-year-old stake races, while Swale was in training for the second tier.

The race in which Swale was to make his debut had only one other horse in it that looked tough. Two days before the race, Shuttle Jet had worked the fastest of any horse at

Belmont Park and was "black lettered" in that day's edition of the *Daily Racing Form*. Swale acted like a kid on the way to the races. Woody didn't believe in schooling a horse in the paddock—I never knew why—so Swale made his debut without the benefit of a rehearsal. He couldn't stop nickering at other horses and was pulling me so strongly that I had to jerk the shank a couple of times to stop him. Once the saddle was put on and Woody's principal jockey, Eddie Maple, was on his back, Swale became much more relaxed. And he was shining. We all bet our lungs on him.

After breaking from the gate, Swale was in a good position, second on the rail. As they were nearing the top of the stretch, the race turned into a match between Shuttle Jet and Swale, with the rest of the pack far behind. Perhaps it was a combination of getting tired and losing heart, or a myriad of other factors facing a racehorse the first time out, but Swale was never able to pass Shuttle Jet. He came in second. "Next time," was all anyone could say.

Next time, two weeks later, Swale was in front the whole way, and never got caught. He returned to the barn as play-ferocious as I had ever seen him. Now Swale knew what it was like alone in front, and he liked it. That win was all Woody Stephens needed. He started to enter Swale in the stake races his pedigree and training down in Aiken all said he belonged in. Breaking the maiden of a horse like Swale was merely a formality.

The horse went on to win two stakes almost immediately, the Breeders Futurity at Keeneland and the Belmont Futurity. After Keeneland, he was considered a legitimate stake horse and could run races that would bring him real money. Of course, this was good for everyone involved with the horse, from the owner down to every groom in the barn. Grooms got one hundred dollars whenever the horse won, while my share of the purse was one percent—a healthy piece of change in every case. From his late season as a two-year-old until his last race, Swale picked up a win check for nothing less than $200,000.

I'm not in the win picture taken after the Belmont Futurity. In the composite made of the victory photos, there's a frame of me leading the horse into the winner's circle, but then there are only images of the owner, the exercise boy, the assistant trainer, and Woody Stephens. I'm missing from the winner's circle—disappeared between frames. I'm looking at it now, twelve years later. What happened to me between the race and the aftermath? I'm probably just outside the frame, outside the winning moment everyone else is experiencing. But it makes sense, too, that I'm trapped in the lapse between the images—daily drinking removed me from them.

Swale's next start was to be in Saratoga Springs. We left Belmont at the end of July for the town I'd had always heard about but had never been to except by way of photographs from the book I'd read on Seattle Slew. The Spa, as it was referred to by practically every horse person, was so idyllic that nothing could prepare you for it. The light was different. There were more trees. And because racing happened here only in August, the barns weren't enclosed the way they were at Belmont. But for me, the beauty of Saratoga was most exemplified by the early morning steam that rose from the barrels of water heating in the backstretch. There was only cold water running through those ancient pipes, so a groom's first task was to fill two barrels and fire them from underneath so there'd be hot water to use in bathing the horses when they came back from the track. Two barrels were usually enough to wash down the morning with. It always felt strange making hot water on hot summer days.

Sometimes, at dusk, Richard and I and some other racetrackers would refill the barrels and cook enough corn to feed the barn. The races had all been run and the betting public had given Saratoga back to the grooms and hotwalkers who were the unofficial guardians of every racetrack night. We would gather at the rail and reminisce. There was something about being in the countryside that made us more sociable, that gave us more time for personal lives. The sight of us standing in the last shadows of trees and barn doors would have looked intimate to a passing stranger. Our collective solitude—what it was in those moments—could bear public witness.

Saratoga was the only track on the New York racing circuit where you could see the races without going to the grandstand. The backstretch of barns ran alongside the backstretch of racecourse. This was a great convenience, but it brought the action up close in a disconcerting way. Horses looked slower, the jocks were very noisy, it all seemed like utter chaos. Again, illusion—what I learned from the Amazing Randi—depended on how far away you were from the stage.

And any shock was personal. There was a wonderful horse called A Phenomenon that was trained by José Rivera. On the turn for home the horse bolted and threw the jockey, Angel Cordero, Jr. The spill occurred at the rail directly across from Woody's barn, and we were all out there, helping Cordero to his feet. A Phenomenon never made it to his feet and had to be put down.

The first year we were stabled at Saratoga, the management put up a building on the backstretch where racetrackers could place bets. As much as this seemed like a racetrack generosity—a rarity—I couldn't help feeling that these windows of parimutuel clerks had been opened to keep us away from the fancy Saratoga crowd. The Spa lived up to its advertising: "the August place to be," especially for the Whitney and Vanderbilt set, an historical conglomerate of money and glamor that had brought as much fame to the month-long meet as had the depth of the racing talent. Still, there was something about Saratoga that made us feel as if we, too, were on vacation, even if it was a working one.

There were huge and great-tasting blue margaritas at the Mexican restaurant outside the back gate, and there was the town itself—gorgeous avenues of architecture, most apparent in the façades of fabled Victorian homes. There was also a swimming pool for racetrackers, and the track kitchen staff (from Aiken, as it turned out) cooked up savory soul food most of the time and served warm iced tea in frosted plastic glasses.

The outfits at Saratoga were in full and glorious display that month. For most stables, these were the most important four weeks in the racing year (also the time for the richest awards in purse money), and trainers went out of their way to make their stable areas showplaces. Careers were made and ended at the Spa. You could come with an unknown quality of racing talent and leave with a much clearer sense of what kind of horse you had.

As for Richard and me, we'd arrived at Saratoga already with a clearer sense of what we had, which wasn't much by this time. We'd stopped having sex down in Aiken. Sex got lost, we used to joke, in the room the tenant had hanged herself in years before we moved into the apartment on Whiskey Road. But sex wasn't exactly gone from the world. With alcohol's help, I managed to get together with two other partners. At a party one night, I'd met a Marine who was leaving for duty the next day. We drank a bottle of Absolut, zigzagged into town, and ended up on the cold and dirty tile floor of a gas station's public bathroom. It was his first time with a guy, he said, and I lied and told him it was mine, too, which thrilled him. We both did so good for something so forbidden, I assured him. We'd been angels in the danger zone.

The other encounter was more bizarre. A wily man who never introduced himself had burst into King's Bar one night, walked up to me, and said that he wanted a blow job. Apart from the flamboyant entrance, what made the scene more fearful was the fact that he knew I was gay despite my never having seen him before. It reminded me of Joseph McCarthy's fifties. How did he know? Having the queer file on someone usually didn't prompt a request for services. It was usually an open invitation to disaster. The comparatively routine homosexual experiences at Belmont were innocuous and seemed, more often than not, to be a result of unbearable heat or too many drugs. While I was ambivalent about the man's sexual desire for me, the potential danger of it was exciting.

We left the bar and I took him to the training track—as quirky and lovely a place I've ever found for what we did. The moon shone blindly. A horse was thrashing in a nearby barn. The man's tongue was bitter. We kissed once, which felt technical to me. He came in my mouth.

Those sexual excursions were so rare and so oddly placed that they never came close in excitement to what the town provided. At Saratoga, most days of the week were spent thinking not about men and sex but about food and money. And the horses.

When you rubbed a good horse for Woody Stephens, you'd usually luck out and have only the one to take care of. But Swale hadn't fully proven himself yet, so I had two other horses as well. One of them, Mia Nordica, sired by the great Northern Dancer but out of a nothing mare, couldn't train and couldn't run. An entity seemed to have entered the filly and couldn't fathom how to possess her. Whatever the problem was, Mia Nordica never got used to my body, either, and being in the stall with her was dangerous, to say the least. She kicked and squealed and hated being handled. Every touch burned her. She was also very loose intestinally, which I kept pointing out to the foreman, but to no avail. It was as though no one was terribly interested in the horse because she had such a wonderful sire. She was a brood mare already—that seemed to be the consensus. What was she doing in a barn full of runners anyway?

My other horse, Arianne Mon Amour, was as skittery as

could be, but smarter and more talented. Arianne had broken her maiden on the grass at Belmont Park, coming from so far out of it that she never made her presence truly felt until the last furlong. To run like that, with that kind of synchronized timing, showed a sophistication rare in a horse so young. She ran once more at Saratoga and won the same way, but she came up with a hairline fracture of the cannon bone and had to be retired.

The Mon Amour sisters—Arianne, Nicole, and Michelle—were all trained by Woody at one time or another. They were named for the three daughters of the man who owned the fillies: Henryk de Kwiatkowski, a multimillionaire whose fortune was made by selling airplanes to Arabs. He was ravishingly handsome. Aside from his trio of fillies—none of which made any serious money—de Kwiatkowski owned the great Conquistador Cielo, the horse that started Woody's great Bel-mont Stakes roll (the trainer won the race five years in a row).

As it happened, with the departure of the two fillies from competition, Swale became the only horse I was taking care of in Saratoga. He was training for the upcoming Saratoga Special.

"He'll win easy. He'll park," Richard beamed.

"Not if he hates the mud."

"Well, his mother was a grass filly—that means a mud lover. He'll win, don't worry. He'll get the lead and never look back."

On the day of the stake, the weather had turned super-natural—electrical and rainy and pitch black. In the primordial slop of an August downpour, Swale ran wire to wire and had a look in his eye afterwards that was new: joy and toughness mixed together. He was sliding into the next status in the racing world, becoming what every handicapper dreads: a favorite.

In the spit box, where I walked Swale luxuriously around, two guys were talking about Devil's Bag.

"Swale's nothing compared to the Bag."

"Right. Bag's a freight train. Swale hasn't got the speed or nearly the tenacity Devil's Bag's got."

I had a kid from Woody's barn who'd followed us back from the winner's circle take Swale a couple of turns and walked over to the two men.

"We'll just see about that, boys," I said, in the straightest voice I could muster.

"See about what?"

"We'll see come Derby Day who the better horse is."

"Shit, come Derby Day, Swale probably won't even be able to run. The way Woody's been entering him in races every two weeks, he won't have anything left. You can see they're saving the Bag. Shit, that horse ain't run since Florida."

"Yeah, that's right, 'cause he's sore," I lied.

"Well, we'll see Derby Day, all right. The Bag will trounce them all."

I took Swale back and finished watering him off, worried, of course. The encounter in the spit box brought back the chill that came with leaving Aiken, when Devil's Bag launched a threat in my mind against the hope I'd had for Swale. While Swale came out of the race fine, I still wasn't so convinced he would fare as well in the upcoming Hopeful Stakes. Track Barron was in the race and he was hard to beat going seven furlongs.

Swale ran third in the Hopeful. No excuses. Again. We'd stopped saying "next time" a race or two ago. Saratoga ended in defeat, but those were important races. Swale was learning what the quality of his competition really was and he was going longer distances—what he'd have to master by Derby Day. As surely as Devil's Bag was being aimed toward the 110th running of the Kentucky Derby, Swale was headed there too and not as a backup this time. He had a legitimate shot at the big race. The only hitch was that Swale now had a pattern of racing that would become his trademark: he almost always followed a win with a loss. The Swale Sandwich, we named it. Poor us, the barn dwellers. And poor handicappers, too. It was a sandwich nobody could wash down with anything.

But something more finite than racing luck was clear to me by the end of the Saratoga meet. Even in his inconsistency, Swale was the most genuine presence in my life. I would always think *honest* when I took him out of the stall to graze next to the barn at feeding time. There was good grass there for a horse, and looking down at him in the dusky August light, head moving over the grass sweetly and carefully, I was always struck by his extraordinary good nature. The sandwich Swale made with his races, the one we were all so critical of, was also the thing that made him such a pleasure to be around. His inconsistency was a reminder that he wasn't simply a running machine. Swale ran with full regard for the thing some trainers will forget about a horse: his heart.

Fourteen

Swale in Mind

After a brief autumn at Belmont, where Swale didn't run, I went down to Florida with him for the races leading up to the Florida Derby. Being back at Hialeah with one of the favorites for the Florida Derby—and the Kentucky Derby, it would turn out—had more range in it. When I look back at the man who was me in Rivera's Argentinian shedrow, I look insecure and green—at the "real" races for the first time with a thirst and hunger to make up for what I didn't know about horsemanship. But mostly, my memory of Florida spirals around my leaving Richard. I had left him again because I had to be on the road with Swale—a demanding but thrilling compensation for not having a lover beside me.

There were times I felt as if I were disappearing with Swale into his languageless domain. He was a listener, and whenever I looked at him alone in the stall, grazing at the end of a shank or running towards victory or defeat, I was always struck by his ability to receive the world simply, without fear or judgment— like a child at that moment of wonder before language answers with the names for things.

Swale's prep races going into the Florida Derby at Gulfstream Park would be the Hutchison Stakes and the Fountain of Youth. Devil's Bag was to run in the Flamingo Stakes, which carried a lot more clout than either of Swale's races. If Swale was to remain true to his form, he'd win the Hutchison and lose the Fountain of Youth, which is exactly what happened. (Devil's Bag lost the Flamingo). But something else happened to Swale when he ran in the Fountain of Youth, something nobody was expecting. He tried to swallow his tongue. For his start in the Florida Derby, Swale's tongue would have to be tied down.

Only on the racetrack will you see a horse with his tongue tied down. The procedure is much easier than it sounds, but it takes two people. One person pulls the tongue as far out of the horse's mouth as it will go. The other takes a swath of white flannel which is about a half an inch wide by one foot long, and places it under the tongue, wraps it once, like a ribbon around a gift, and finishes off the procedure with a bow tie under the horse's chin. The tongue is held in place under the bit of the bridle, preventing the horse from swallowing it. I didn't know why a horse would try to swallow his tongue, and nobody I asked knew either. It probably has something to do with the tight hold the jockey has on him, or a habit of taking in too much air.

Because Devil's Bag and Swale were two tributaries leading to the same river in Louisville, Kentucky, the media spent their best headlines on them. Woody's rapport with Howard Cosell, Douglas Kiker, and other television sports personalities was legend, but he was not well versed in other kinds of media: *People* magazine or *Vanity Fair,* for example. Someone had profiled Woody in *People,* and he claimed he had never heard of the magazine. When *Vanity Fair* sent Annie Leibovitz down to photograph Devil's Bag, Woody made his position on the print media even clearer. Leibovitz was going to rig a gray velvet curtain between some trees, much in the same way she had photographed Baryshnikov in an arabesque atop a grand piano. But Woody wouldn't hear of it. He said the whole thing would excite the horse too much, and he sent Leibovitz and her crew back to New York.

As funny as the story was at the time, it revealed something wonderful about Stephens's sense of priorities. Horses were king, and coverage by a partial judge, like the media, didn't interest him. What I had initially taken as a flair for media attention as a whole was actually selective. Woody was only interested in the television coverage—because it was wider in scope?—and there was certainly enough of it that winter of 1984. But it was the story that came out in *Sports Illustrated,* written by William Nack, called "He's Got the Horse Right Here" that had everyone in the barn so excited. Even Woody had to admit it was the best piece ever written about him. That story gave me insight into a Woody Stephens that I hadn't gleaned from any of my encounters with him on those late afternoons, after the races, back at the barn:

. . ."And I'll always remember that morning at Havre de Grace racetrack, when we worked those two horses in the dark in the rain."

Woody didn't say this so much as mutter it, as if in a moment of free association, between something he had just said and something he was about to say. It seemed at the time a line too quick and lovely to chase, something best left alone, a metaphor that somehow expressed a sense of the poetry, chance and excitement of life as he had lived it on American racetracks since he was a boy.

It suggested a daguerreotype of what was in his mind. You know . . . It rained one early morning in Maryland, at Havre de Grace, and Woody sped through it, in the dark, flat around the turn, a very young man hunched over the back of a horse that's no longer alive, on a racetrack that no longer exists—the horse breathing hard, his hooves striking and splashing beneath him, the wind and water in the rider's face and the horse carrying him very fast through the stretch toward home, to wherever.

Nack had a lovely way of talking about Stephens. His was the first piece I had read about the sport of horse racing that meant a lot to me as a writer. Here was a way to talk about the racetrack that wasn't filled with jargon or knowledge about a life only a racetracker could acquire. Nack had turned the track and Woody's part in it into poetry.

Stephens never let anyone stand between him and that moment of public recognition, or they'd hear about it. After Swale won the Saratoga Special, Eddie Maple, the jockey, looked down at me and said: "How far did we win by?" "A couple of lengths," I said. Woody barged in with, "You shut up now!" It wasn't that I was wrong but that I was standing in the sun for a minute too long. This was one of his great moments in racing, and the sound of one of his help trilling over the cheering crowd caught him off guard. And it was a reminder he didn't need: a drunken groom scratching on the freshly smoothed surface of a triumph.

"He'll park," Big Dave said about Swale's chances in the Florida Derby. Big Dave was a Woody groupie who worked for other outfits around the track but was always showing up at the barn a day or so before one of our big races. Dave and I were at the grandstand at Gulfstream Park—a grandstand that looked like a motel lobby with betting windows in it. I had just given Swale over to the pony girl, and Dave and I stood there squinting in the outrageously bright day into our draught beers. I didn't like the beer from any racetrack concession stand. Aside from the bad quality of the lager, the paper cups it came in were flimsy and the stuff got warm too quickly. The beer tasted the way it smells spilled over the seats in a car.

Again, as it had been with the Hopeful Stakes, I was not so convinced that Swale would park. He was coming into the race after his predestined defeat in the Fountain of Youth

Stakes and even though, according to the sandwich theory, we were home free this time, there was always a variable or two that hung in the air. I hadn't really traveled with Swale enough yet to know how vanning would effect his performance—that was one variable. The other was a horse named Dr. Carter, a gray speedball of John Veitch's that could certainly provide Swale with tough competition if he wasn't as sore as he was rumored to be.

Dr. Carter was sore that day; Swale caught him easily at the wire. In the photograph taken after the race, I am standing with my horse in the winner's circle dressed in a silk shirt that has the Chinese character for luck sewn shakily inside a red square. But Swale is better dressed: otherworldly black and glinting in the sun, statuesque under his purple blanket of lavish victory orchids.

Keeneland. One last Kentucky Derby prep.

Keeneland Racetrack in Lexington, Kentucky, is different from other tracks. Its paddock is unusually close to the racing strip, but more unusual is the fact that Keeneland is the only racetrack in America without a track announcer. Horses run there through a silence that feels like prestige. You, the devotee apparent, are expected to know the barn the horse is from by the jockey's silk color—Lexington is horse country, after all. Without the announcer's voice, the race looks more like a stampede. Part of the comfort of the racing call, I realized, is imagining that the narration is actually responsible for the outcome.

Another notable characteristic of Keeneland is the attitude taken toward public intoxication. Decorum was valued almost

as highly as the horses were. At the end of every racing day
patrons who were walking funny were picked up and loaded
into a van bound for the county jail—where I was soon to
spend a restless night. Less than a week after my arrival in
Lexington, I was at a clubhouse party being given for owners
and trainers. I can't remember how, as a common groom, I was
ever allowed into the celebration, but I was. After insulting
John Veitch (I don't remember what I said) and telling Dale
Hancock, Swale's co-owner, that I was in love with her, I was
either thrown or got pushed into Martha Lane Collins—then
the governor of Kentucky—and my drink flew into her face. I
was in a blackout which got interrupted long enough for me
to remember being escorted away by uniformed men from the
open bar and the banquet table surrealistically awash in shiny
crawfish.

After being dropped off at the barn, I proceeded to down
a pint of vodka and yell curses at the Pinkerton guards as they
walked in the dark road around the stable area. Twenty minutes later, that famous van, bound for jail, pulled up and swal-
lowed me whole.

I'd been in prison one other time in my life, for sleeping
on a sand dune in Provincetown, Massachusetts. The incar-
ceration lasted one night, and my stepfather, in a rare act of
generosity, wired money to pay for my bus trip back to New
York. But the Lexington stretch wasn't as scenic because the
charge was different. And I was terrified, thrown suddenly
into the real world in one of its worst variations. From the
drunk tank, I looked through the bars into the next cell where
a body builder was lifting weights. When I wasn't feeling

attracted to him, he scared me. It was odd, seeing something I'd seen in the outside world being reenacted behind bars—as strange as watching somebody vacuum the street or prepare dinner in an alleyway. Weightlifting made jail look domestic when it was domesticity's opposite.

Jail called me once before in my life, but I didn't have to go. I had stolen an automobile when I was a student at Bennington College. The keys were in the ignition of Georgia M.'s car and I figured I'd only take the old Valiant down to the covered bridge and back. I was drunk and managed in very little time to crash the car into a tree and leave the scene of the accident. A shattered windshield got tangled in my blood-soaked hair. I had suffered only minor scrapes and bruises, nothing considering what should have become of me; the car ended up bent like an accordion around an old maple tree.

I made it to the main road and hitched a ride back to campus, but any hope I had of not being attached to the crime faded in that first hour when I was picked up by a patrol cop slowly scanning the deserted Vermont night. Of course, he couldn't see through me or to the covered bridge or further to the tree the car had died around, so he didn't connect me to anything yet. He knew only that I was out late and drunk—not so unusual for a student from the weird college up the hill. When the same cop and his partner came knocking on my dormitory door early the next morning, I knew the jig was up.

I almost went to jail, but grand larceny was ruled out when Georgia decided not to press charges. However, the crime of leaving the scene of an accident was still on the docket. By the time the case actually made it into court, it was sum-

mer and I was living with a professor at Bennington named
Frank Baker whom I was helping recover from a stroke. Frank
told me to mention his name to the judge, and when I did, the
judge smiled and dropped the remaining charge.

Frank Baker smiled, too, when I got home and told him
what had happened in court. But the smile was his only
response. Frank wouldn't give an explanation for the judge's
decision, and I didn't press it—pressing it would have been
like asking the rainbow for one more color.

They really do trade food for cigarettes in jail, so I went to
trial a very hungry groom on the morning of my arraignment.
Unbeknownst to me, Claiborne had sent Michael Grimes down
with a station wagon, which was waiting to take me back to
racehorses. Michael Grimes was the yearling manager at
Claiborne, and while he didn't know it yet, he'd be joining the
outfit in the next two weeks to help with Swale's training.
Woody would be in the hospital, suffering with emphysema and
two broken ribs sustained after a fall at home in his bathtub.

"How did they treat you in jail?" Grimes asked.

"Okay, I guess. I kept saying Swale was going to win the
Derby."

"Did they believe you?"

"Nope, not the ones who knew what a Swale is. Do you
think he'll win?"

But Grimes didn't answer. He kept driving through the
dense landscape of rolling hills that had long ago turned into
the thriving horse farms Lexington was famous for. Grimes's
silence at the wheel made me think of my stepfather who'd
kept driving after our olden day at the races—a memory now

blinded by a spectacular sunset so that I couldn't see my step-father's face at all but could feel the heat of his lust for gambling and sex, the forces that were driving him.

Grimes was surprisingly cool during that short trip back to the racetrack. He'd never liked me. Grimes was a cowboy, and I wasn't like anyone he'd met before. More than being outside sexual acceptability, I said what I thought, which bothered him. But now I wasn't talking much; I was too worried I'd be fired. The closer we got to Keeneland, the more convinced I was that Grimes was hiding the eviction notice from me. *Which groom would get to have Swale?*

There'd been a lot of jealousy surrounding me and the horse from the very beginning. When Swale went off to Keeneland for the first time, as a two-year-old, to run in the Breeders Futurity, Harold Rigby went with him. I wasn't road-experienced, so I stayed home, and Rigby, the tall Jamaican groom from Barn Three, was sure Woody Stephens would put Swale into one of his stalls as soon as the two returned victorious from the blue hills. But it didn't happen, and Harold resented me from then on. Perhaps his jealousy (and that of other grooms as well) was caused by the fact that everyone felt I hadn't been with Woody long enough to deserve this. To all the oldtimers who'd been with Woody for years, it must have seemed as if I'd figured out the combination to his safe.

Woody Stephens stood in the middle of the shedrow at Keeneland, waiting for me. It was a gray afternoon the day I was sprung, and the grayness made the horses and the people look as if they were moving slower. I walked toward Woody, dazed from words I heard in my head, the words I'd heard him say before to a reckless groom: "I don't believe I can use you anymore."

"What the hell is wrong with you?" Stephens said instead.

"I don't know, Woody. I fucked up. I'm sorry."

"Straighten up. Your problem is you miss that boy in New York. We're here for the reason, not the season."

What Woody said about Richard was true, but hearing it, particularly from him, was startling. I'd figured Woody knew I was gay, but to make a comment this intimate was out of character. Whatever adversity he may have been conscious of on his shedrow (and there was plenty of it), Woody never acknowledged it directly.

It was true. I did miss Richard—talking to him, mostly. But we didn't do well on the phone. Besides, a phone was a luxury on the track, the way mail was a luxury. On the racetrack, the only people you encountered were the ones you saw every day. What could I have said to Richard? Ending up in jail was too reminiscent of so many drunken missteps I'd taken back in New York. Richard had run out of patience with me long ago, and he wasn't likely to take me in his arms for comfort. He probably would have said, "For God's sake, when is enough enough? Stop drinking!" I didn't want to hear that advice just then or get that scolding. "Stop drinking" was always the obvious solution, the bumper sticker on the car in front of me. And the brick wall that, with my own fiery self-will, I had always managed to drive straight through.

I went to Swale's stall as soon as Woody left the barn and talked to him for a few minutes—standing back to see what he looked like through the filter of my own recklessness. I cried into his huge, black neck and just kept telling him I wouldn't go anywhere anymore. I'd stay until the Derby, at least until the Derby. Who knew after that? I was still drinking and couldn't make any long-term promises.

In Swale's stall I remembered something about my mother. She was in St. Vincent's Hospital after suffering her first nervous breakdown—long before the breakdown that put her in the marriage to the man who didn't like women. My natural father, with an impeccable sense of timing, had asked my mother for $25,000, money she had from an old inheritance. If she refused him, he'd start with divorce proceedings, he said.

My mother didn't give him a penny, and after their separation I assumed that when one parent left the family, the other one wasn't far behind. I thought parents did what some animals I'd seen on television did—leave their young howling alone in the world for the rest of time.

And then it happened. It was the week of John Kennedy's presidential election, and I woke up one night to my mother missing. She had taken an overdose of sleeping pills and casually walked down to Bellevue Hospital, where she had her stomach pumped. My mother decided not to die that night, but my brother and I had been abandoned. As a child, abandonment had the same unreal effect death would have had—a failed trick, stumping even the Amazing Randi, with the disappeared not coming back. In that concrete stall at Keeneland, I felt that I had just done to Swale what my mother had done to me—walked away from the living thing I was given to care for. The realization paralyzed me just long enough to make me feel that I had to protect what I loved, no matter how much I drank.

The garlic wreaths over the stalls in Florida had shown me that superstition played a part when it came to racehorses. Now superstition was working in my favor: because I had done well by the horse and hadn't gotten into serious trouble up until then, Woody was reluctant to break up the winning combination of horse and groom. I had been saved by a hardboot grace everyone on the track said got bred in Kentucky. What I didn't know then was that hard-boot grace was a kind of lightning that struck only once.

In a day or so, the gray and lingering effect of jail was replaced by something sunnier. It looked as if Swale could win the Lexington Stakes laughing. For one thing, his competition had taken other roads to the Derby, and there was virtually no talent in the race. The track came up sloppy—what one race-tracker referred to as having "the consistency of toothpaste on a desktop." The track's condition didn't worry me too much after I remembered how well Swale had handled the mud at Saratoga. The only problem was that the race fell on the bad half of his win/lose pattern.

And the problem followed him into the starting gate. A horse named He Is a Great Deal took the lead and never looked back. That horse was on lighter fluid. Swale came in second. Nevertheless, newspaper photographers crowded around and took pictures anyway as we left the track. Under his cooler, Swale was covered in mud. He looked sore. I looked sore, too. My sunglasses were dappled with mud. There was a mud sky. We walked toward the cameras, both with looks of wonder mixed with awful defeat.

We left Keeneland losers: Swale, a star a little lowered in

the racetrack sky, came into the Derby off a bad second-place finish. And I was a public intoxicant now, jailed for something I was good at—for something I thought all along had been keeping me free. I'd been miserable at Keeneland: jail, the Lexington loss, virtually no one to talk to, and with what was still my heart in that particular junction of desperation and fear of the unknown, I missed *that boy* in New York.

But I also knew that Richard and I were at an ending. What had started out at River Downs as a kind of experiment had changed us into seasoned racetrackers, and we'd been nullified in a way. We were not the same idealistic couple that once rode the Staten Island Ferry back and forth, or the couple sitting up long nights drinking tea in the apartment, smoking cigarettes, listening to songs on the piano, making love.

Now I kept leaving Richard behind while I went in search of fame, glory, and sometimes even self-respect in the racing world, leaving without talking first about my solo flight on the wings of a horse. Not acknowledging Swale in that way may well have been what most confounded the relationship between my lover and me and kept it from ever being wholly transformed. The way it felt in my body was that Richard and I had been stuck with each other for too long.

And Swale provided the counterpoint to that stasis. I loved the horse more than anything, yet I also knew he was the screen onto which I was projecting what was possible, not inevitable, in my life. The problem was that while good things were happening to Swale and me, they were not happening within me. As much happiness as I felt around Swale, I knew it was temporary. He changed my life in many ways, but he didn't change *me*. So much of what I thought about myself remained remarkably the same.

The tragic flaw in the relationship between horse and groom was that the only way I could deal with Swale's success was by toasting to it. If nothing else, Lexington County Jail provided me with substantial proof that all along I had been making toasts to Swale with every drink the world would let me have.

Fifteen

Swale in Time

I had been to Churchill Downs before. In some interlude hard to locate in time—more like a taste or a temperature—but probably during the early eighties, I was working for Buddy and Jewel Fisk. They were at Churchill to run a couple of horses one month—a break from Beulah Park. I was taking a horse over to the paddock for the third race, drinking a 3.2 percent beer and then putting a Camel out in it. I was eating biscuits and gravy in the track kitchen and walking into town at night to discover what tilted it, if anything like a gay scene tilted it. There was a good gay bar: Discovery, I think it was called. It was large and warm, with a spongy dance floor and wood paneling. Being there was like being inside a coffin.

Isn't cruising like a death scene sometimes? So many men standing around perfectly still and expressionless, except for a dark spark in the eyes because they are mind reading and crotch- and body-they-can't-see-reading. They are trying to figure out if they would want to be with someone like you when you are naked. *That* balanced on top of calculating if you would like to be with them naked. I wonder what they think about more: themselves or you?

I picked up one of the boys who did the strip show. He was close to me in age and open and funny. He turned in huge, voluptuous circles from the hips down, like a snake inside a drum. He liked my voice. He thought I was funny. I wondered if, when he was cruising me, he was thinking that I was funny; if funny enters the death stare the cruise is locked inside.

I took him back to the track. His name was Cary and he had never seen a racehorse before, except on television.

"Do they all sleep like that, standing up?

"No, the good ones lie down, to save the legs."

We entered the tack room. An alcohol smell came off the horse blankets. And there were various tools of the trade: bridles and halters and saddles, of course, but also things a layperson wouldn't know: a twitch, the disciplinary device that looks like a billy club with a ring of chain link on the end to twist around the horse's upper lip to make it stand still for the blacksmith or the vet; epsom salts for soaking feet in; fish oil that murkied-up coffee cans and got brushed on hooves to promote growth; cribbing straps (the equine equivalent of a neck brace) to keep a horse from getting at the bandages on his legs. There were muzzles to keep a horse from ingesting anything the night before a race, and blinkers, satin masks with plastic shields cupped around the eyes to block the peripheral vision of a horse that is particularly distracted by knowing he has company.

Cary was fascinated with the strangeness of the equipment, and wanted to know every minute: *What's that for?*

"Not for where we're going," I answered, wrestling him down to the floor.

We had a hurried, cramped kind of sex because we were surrounded by horse gear—the smell and shine and nonuse of it. And the more we went at it, the stranger the whole scene became to Cary. He was laughing between the lunges with his tongue into my bellybutton and started knocking the tack around, dropping the saddle off its stand and finally getting his legs tangled up in the shanks and bridles that were hanging over our heads.

And there was rain in and out of our knocking around, rain that got mixed in with the alcohol smell from the blankets and the chewing tobacco smell in Cary's mouth. For Cary, it may have been all the horse tack that established the scene. But for me, used to horses, it was the rain. It moved through everything with a sound like a curtain opening and closing, and it made the sex seem timeless.

"I've never been around so much leather," Cary joked as we walked out the main gate at 4:00 A.M.

Churchill Downs was just starting to rustle again, and cars slushed through the backstretch made muddy overnight by rain. The morning voices under the shedrow were rising in excitement about the day's card of races. A South African man at Bill Mott's stable was carrying on so loudly about a horse in the third race that the foreman had to hand over a horse he was walking in order to go over and find out what the odds were.

That South African man in a leading trainer's barn is one of the last images I have of the Churchill Downs that came before this Churchill Downs. In 1984, there was no South African, no walk to a gate in the city with a stripper under the Louisville moon, dancing like a snake inside a drum, slithering out and across the floor of a coffin. There was no sex or tack room washed through with rain. And Bill Mott's barn had changed into stall after stall of even better horses.

On Churchill nights now, I went out and aimlessly pulled wildflowers on my way through the main gate, putting one behind my ear—another kind of ritual, like the one with a knife in Aiken, to evoke renown. I hit the bar and drank until I passed out in front of the Joker Poker machine or fell, laughing, into the arms of a woman in a uniform whom I should have known by name but whom I affectionately referred to as Pinky Pinkerton. Pinky had walked me home one night early in the racing meet and by now this walk had become a routine. Pinky, my Derby-groom bodyguard.

I had my own room with a cot in it and a wonderfully strange-looking Sony tape player I had bought with part of my earnings from Swale's Young America victory. It looked like a red industrial battery. A few days later, I would pawn that machine for fifty bucks to bet on Swale, because on Derby Day I was broke. Dressed up, excited, a little drunk. And broke.

One night, after vomiting all over the door to my room, I started praying to Swale for help in getting sober. Toasting to his success suddenly seemed counterproductive, and the whole track was delirious with Derby fever, which I had, too. As each day unfolded and we were moving closer to the "reason and not the season," I was becoming excited by the possibility of Swale's moving us all up into the stratosphere—which is what a Derby win would mean. But I was terrified too, not by his possible defeat but by the fact of my own, unstoppable drunkenness. The prayer to Swale sounded like a plea for sobriety, but in retrospect it was a request for a star's greatest performance. His chances—as they had always been for the last two years—were far greater than mine ever were.

Devil's Bag had come to Churchill, too, but with his stunning defeat in the Flamingo Stakes at Hialeah, Swale had begun to emerge through the Devil's monumental shadow— never as a faster horse than the Bag, but more the artful one. Swale ran just fast enough to win.

Old racetrack adage: Time matters only in jail.

And speed can finish a thoroughbred, too. Every triumph is a kind of fracture, and the stress can cause a horse to decline when he should be seasoning. One afternoon, speed finished the Bag. Veterinarians found a bone chip in the right knee after Devil's Bag's warm-up race at Churchill, and he went home to begin stud duty, leaving the whole racing world focused now, once and for all, on Swale.

The morning of the 110th running of the Kentucky Derby was steel gray and soft and humid, a morning that made you feel as if you were standing inside an engine that couldn't hurt you—an engine that hadn't been unpacked. All of Woody Stephens's stable were planted in front of Stall Three, Derby Barn, looking at the big horse. Swale. He looked ready. Fresh. Famous.

And we already figured we'd each be getting a lapel-flower from the luscious victory blanket of American Beauty roses that came with the money, the trophy, and the garbage can filled with Moët champagne on ice. Swale was the horse to beat—I knew that, and so did that morning's *Daily Racing Form*. Every handicapper picked him to win, if I remember right. I thought that Swale could have beaten Devil's Bag, if the Bag had been running, but I kept the thought to myself because to say anything would have been a signal to the outfit that I wasn't loyal to its greater good, that I wasn't a team player.

Under the dream of a sparkling future, however, was a wave of worry. Swale's workout a couple of days earlier had been disappointing and had made Woody Stephens a little nervous. It was just too slow. What made us all little more hopeful was the early speed variable. Wayne Lucas's horse Althea, the only filly in the race, would probably charge right to the front, which would set it up just perfectly for our horse to make his debonair late move.

Other than Althea, Swale's running mates were not an incredibly talented bunch. He was always burying softer horses. And what horses were left were very often also being trained by Woody Stephens. Theoretically, Swale's toughest opponent had always been Devil's Bag, a horse he would never actually run against.

It was almost time to take owner Seth Hancock's favorite horse over to the paddock, so I ducked under the rubber tie that kept Swale in his stall and started running vet-wrap. Vet-wrap is something like an Ace bandage, but an adhesive on the back goes against the skin and it's as thin as paper. Swale had run down a couple of times in earlier races—hitting front, back or all four ankles on the track—so we weren't taking any chances. We would also tie his tongue down. Since he had showed us before running in the Florida Derby that the procedure annoyed him, we waited until the last minute—the fuzziest one for all of us, the pressure on—while Swale stood, already saddled, in the paddock.

Swale needed the tongue-tie to run, but little else. In some earlier races, he had looked as if he was trying to bear out a little and we had tried putting a burr on him—a device that looks like a small circular scrub brush. The burr gets fastened to the right side of the bit and pushes against the mouth to keep the horse from drifting to the outside rail. But, for some reason, the burr seemed to be needed only when we were running at Saratoga.

Swale was perfectly cool on his walk over to the Churchill paddock, past the huge crowd of eager onlookers who were drinking and screaming and jumping up and down, softly and all in slow motion. This was the largest crowd of racing fans Swale would see his whole racing life—well-wishers at the gate of possible immortality. Earlier that week, someone told me that a horse sees a magnified version of us, and I couldn't help thinking Swale must have been convinced that day that the world had been invaded by giants. And they all knew his name. What made him feel protected from all that? I was amazed that so many people didn't faze him. A horse is prepared in many ways for a race, but there is no dress rehearsal for the actual walk to the paddock, complete with thousands who cheer. He was the favorite on the way over, but by race time he'd gone down to co-favorite. Everybody had bet the farm on Althea.

As I said, I was broke on Derby Day, and the outfit I was wearing (chinos with white shirt and yellow tie) had been provided to me by Dale Hancock. I felt grateful but also ashamed. Cold, suddenly. Why was I broke? Why didn't I know how to dress for an occasion? Here I was in the one arena everyone on the racetrack dreams about. How did I get here? Throughout the journey from Florida to New York and back, with horses and with Richard coming and going, there had always been something steady shining down the road—the part of life that doesn't drown in the river of booze—but something more. Still, I didn't know what was leading me, the way I didn't know what kind of power it was that Frank Baker had over a small-town judge. Swale was the answer, but what was the question? It certainly wasn't whether I'd win Richard back. Not anymore.

Any sense to be made of my standing in Louisville, Kentucky, probably got born in Aiken, South Carolina. There, in that sleepy section of the South, the first real changes of my racetrack life were shifting into place: Richard and me drifting apart, two sudden deaths, Nick Reston, and finally Swale's appearance in all of our lives.

And if it was a renewed kind of hope that was born too, in Aiken, it came with the thought that I finally wanted to do something right. If I couldn't keep the relationship with Richard or stop grieving over my mother's death or stifle the anger at my stepfather for his abuse towards me and checking into a hospital when he should have been checking on my mother, I could at least finish a journey with a horse. My journeys with people had all started to feel like shocks to the system.

The consistency of taking Swale from stake to stake meant that time was not just a series of fragments strung together through sunlight and moonlight. Incest fragmented time. Alcohol fragmented it, too, as did mental illness and death. But now, just before Woody Stephens was about to tie Swale's tongue down, I could feel the fullness of present time as it included me. For that one moment, under the ancient swinging paddock lights off the main street in Louisville, Kentucky, I was exactly where I was meant to be.

I was listening to the instructions delivered by Mike Grimes to Laffit Pincay, the jockey, on how to run the race. Eddie Maple, Swale's usual rider, had committed himself to Devil's Bag back in Florida, and was without a Derby mount. For Pincay, the recurring instruction was always this simple: Stay close to the pace and don't move until you have to. The instruction always swept me away. It seemed obvious that Woody was talking to the horse.

After leading Swale around the paddock for a couple of turns, I took him down to the racing strip of Churchill Downs, which, in my mind, had turned into the most dazzling strip of racetrack in the United States. After handing the horse over to the pony that gave him to the post parade that gave him to the starting gate that was about to give him to all of us, I looked around for someone from the outfit to watch the race with, but I couldn't find a soul. The more I thought about it, not finding anyone was probably a good thing. Great moments are more fully felt alone.

I knew I had the best horse in the world, and he was due for a win. He looked grand, which, if I ever got lost in worry, would be all the redemption I ever needed. One turn of the head and it all came back: Swale was as consistently a good-looking horse as there ever was. He always looked the part, as I rarely did.

"And they're off!" Mike Battaglia, the track announcer said.

Althea took the early lead, as predicted by everyone on the backstretch. Around the far turn, Althea was still in front with Swale lying third. Coax Me Chad, outrun to the far turn, was now moving through along the inside, while Gate Dancer, who broke poorly from his outside post position, was racing wide but advancing. Swale was starting to move up as he headed toward the turn. Fali Time, never far back, was coming on into the stretch while Pine Circle made up some ground approaching the final furlong. Fight Over, well placed into the backstretch, was moving along the inside nearing the far turn and racing forwardly into the stretch, but then he brushed with At the Threshold. Swale was in front now, flying with Laffit Pincay into the part of time that didn't have any horses in it. He was running easy and if he didn't fall down he was going to win the 110th running of the Kentucky Derby,

Churchill Downs, Louisville, Kentucky. Weather: Steel gray and humid. Time: About 5:30. Date: May 5, 1984.

But there was still the finish line. And I started watching *it* instead of the race—gazing hard at its solemnity and its stillness, its function as a margin on a page of steamrolling horses. I was fixated on the finish line, all of it stretched thin and black across the brown cushion of racetrack. How could it look so insubstantial—almost invisible if you weren't looking from the right angle—and still mean everything?

When Woody Stephens walked into the directors' room at Churchill Downs to watch the race on television, he told a reporter he felt "So-so at best." He had come to the track in a limousine from the hospital where he was still recuperating. As Woody watched Swale stalk Althea, he was getting more and more excited. A local paper the next day quoted Woody as saying: "He'll win by five. They'll all back up behind her."

Which is exactly what happened. As soon as Swale took the lead with three or four furlongs to go, it was all over. He was running easily, under a hand ride, with little urging, but I couldn't bear to watch the actual finish. I looked up at the sky at the moment Swale crossed the line, praying that he'd come back in one piece—that the race hadn't taken too much out of him.

The crowd went wild (5 to 2 are good odds), and I ran down to the track terrified that in all the post-race frenzy I wouldn't be able to get to Swale in time to take him back to the spit box. He was precious cargo now. Pincay came back to the winner's circle, ecstatic and silent. Swale was beside himself. It was as if he actually knew what had just happened— that the eighth race at Churchill Downs on the first Saturday in May carried more importance than any other race in his life. The horse was glistening, and I practically pulled his head down to my heart so he could hear it.

The flurry of activity—flashbulbs from a sea of cameras—inside and outside the winner's circle was like being at a film première. People seemed to appear out of nowhere, and I had to forge my way through an oncoming wave of fans and track officials. Reporters were asking me questions I didn't have time to answer because I had to get Swale back to the spit box and start watering him off. Derby or no Derby, it was still a horse race and I had to take care of my horse.

Seth Hancock came backstage a little disheveled and very happy. He gave us all, the barn help, some money for a victory dinner, but it was only enough money for a first round of drinks, according to my calculations. Before leaving the barn, Hancock announced that Swale would run in the Preakness, if he had pulled through the Derby sound.

We went to a bar. I remember a man was singing Dan Fogelberg's "Run for the Roses." And I cried in that town's public darkness and walked with the crew down the dawn-wet streets of what Louisville was when you won the Kentucky Derby. It wasn't much of a town, but it didn't matter. Horse racing had changed my mind into a pool of sparkling hope: *Triple Crown,* it kept saying. Nothing bad could happen in a world suddenly blazing with three points in a crown.

Sixteen

In Swale Time

Publicity around a horse is like a fire in a mine: You never know what it will light up in the dark. You can build press around the past performances of a horse to some degree, but as any professional horseman will tell you, the game is not guaranteed by intellect or by what the records might say. Like public opinion swaying at an actor's next performance, a horse truly is only as good as the last race he was in.

When the van from the airport carrying Swale and me

fresh from Churchill Downs arrived at Pimlico Racetrack in Baltimore, everyone who gathered to greet the horse was wearing a baseball cap with the same prediction block-lettered in shiny black letters: HAVE A SWALE PREAKNESS. I felt my heart sinking before I even made it down the ramp. The hats weren't a good sign. The Preakness track favored speed horses, and Swale, as he had proven again and again, was not a speed horse. It was the consensus of most of us in the barn that Swale was running the race only because the Preakness was a jewel in the Crown, and to fulfill a theoretical obligation, he had to make a showing. The last jewel—the Belmont Stakes— was much more to his taste, both in terms of distance and quality of racing surface. Swale liked it slow, and he liked running most of his races at home.

One day, Reggie Jackson came to the barn to see the horse. I'd been alerted to his arrival, though it didn't make too much of an impression on me. I hate baseball. When Jackson arrived, I said, "I guess you're here to see Swale," to which he replied: "Well, when they come to the ballpark, they come to see me."

After Jackson left the barn, I got drunk, and in the two weeks at Pimlico, drinking was all that was left of me. All the prayers to Swale to keep me sober had remained untranslatable. How could I ever think a horse, or the love for one, could break an addiction? I was speaking in tongues now: howling down the shedrow at ghosts, and I was louder and even more obnoxious than usual. Something in my drinking life was changing. It was as if someone had told me I only had a certain amount of time left, and I had to drink even more to compensate for it.

One night after downing a pint of Southern Comfort and a six-pack of Heineken—an effective drunk invented in Aiken—I pissed all over my tack room, ripped up books, and proceeded to stomp up and down the shedrow screaming at the guards who should have been watching Swale but who were playing cards instead. I don't know what I said exactly— the string of blackout fragments wasn't as important as what the sun shone down on the next morning. Woody Stephens marched into the barn on May 16, 1984, to fire me, once and for all.

On the afternoon of the day before I was let go, Steve Crist from the *New York Times* asked me: "So did you ever dream you'd be grooming a Derby horse?" On a plane out of Baltimore, I read the piece he'd written—by now a kind of ghost story:

Renaissance Man Takes Care of Swale
Special to *The New York Times*

BALTIMORE, Md., May 16—Every morning for the last two months, Michael Klein has heard the same questions: How is your horse? Is he feeling good? How did he sleep and eat today?

As groom and closest companion of Swale, the colt who won the Kentucky Derby 11 days ago, Klein is expected to know the answers to those questions, and he does, answering them with a cool but professional reserve. He also has his own questions, especially for visitors from New York, and they have little to do with feeding and rubbing a horse.

Klein wants to know: What do you hear about the new Stephen Sondheim musical? And what about that new poet who was supposed to be published in *The New Yorker?* And who's playing at the Village Gate this week?

It isn't that Klein is not interested in his immediate surrounds, but that he has lived in and sees beyond the world of the race track. Even seeing his colt win the Derby, the dream of everyone who has ever owned, trained or rubbed a horse, has not tempted him to put blinkers on his own interests and ambitions.

"I guess I'm not what people think of as the typical groom," he says with a wry smile of understatement. "Grooms are supposed to say 'Yes, sir' and 'No, sir' a lot and whistle while they work and talk to their horses. That's not me."

It certainly isn't. If Klein whistles while he works, it's likely to be a few bars of one of his own compositions or maybe something by the jazz artist Al Jarreau—"Swale really liked him as a baby."

Klein, who is 30 years old, has been around Swale longer than any of the colt's other handlers, having cared for him since the colt was a yearling in December 1981 and went with a dozen other Claiborne Farm yearlings from that nursery in Lexington, Ky., to a training center in Aiken, S.C. Klein's own route to the race track was far less typical.

Born in Washington, Klein grew up in New York City as a precocious Upper West Side teen-aged Bohemian. His friends were the sons and daughters of actors and artists, and he was a budding poet and writer while he attended Columbia Grammar School and later, Music and Art High.

He went to Bennington College in Vermont, studying English, music and dance. Then, after three years, like any self-respecting artiste, he moved to New York's Greenwich Village.

"Any time I had three dollars in my pocket I took a dance

class," he says, "but that wasn't too often. I had a pretty good band going, and we played at the Village Gate and Tramps and s.n.a.f.u. I also got a scholarship to the New Dance Group and studied dance with Laura Dean and Merce Cunningham, but I got too fat to dance and decided to change my life."

His best friend's father was a "gypsy trainer" with a string of horses at River Downs in Ohio, and Klein got a job there as a hotwalker. He eventually landed at Hialeah, where he became a groom for the trainers José Rivera and John Veitch.

He came north with those outfits and, one day in May 1981, heard from a pony girl at Belmont Park that Woody Stephens needed a groom. He got the job on the basis of his references and was given three horses to rub. By December, all of them had broken down or been retired, and Klein was sent to Claiborne to accompany the yearlings to Aiken. One of the horses put under his care was a colt by Seattle Slew out of Tuerta.

"They didn't think too much of him at first," Klein remembers, "because he was over at the knees—his knee stuck out over his cannon bone."

"He's a really easy colt to take care of," says Klein, "because he's so sound and sensible. He's broken my glasses twice and bit me a couple of times, but that's nothing compared to most horses."

Even the thrill and rewards of the Derby victory, however, have not made him any more likely to stay on the track much longer. He wants to get back around the New York music scene, he wants to compose some songs, including one about Swale, and he hopes to write some fiction.

"I don't want to train,'" he says. "I wouldn't be good at having people work for me. I'm too much of an anarchist. When I was a choreographer, my dancers hated me. But the track isn't that far removed from art. People have visions. Woody has visions of what he wants his horses to be and I like being part of that."

Pretty sunny, for a guy who'd just been fired.

Of course, this hadn't been the first time I was fired from a job for being a drunk. When I was a student at Bennington, I lived and worked one semester in Philadelphia during what the school calls a non-resident term. This was a requirement, the college's way of giving you a taste of the real world before you had to live in it.

Philadelphia had been a very saturated time for me. I'd been breaking up with a high-school girlfriend and was overlapping into another kind of sexuality. And I was drinking like crazy. I lived in Germantown, in a huge house with a bunch of other people who'd all been friends at Bennington. The house was owned by a group therapist who insisted everyone partake in his weekly sessions—part of the deal for living in the house. I was working at the Philadelphia Museum of Art in the museum shop office, which was upstairs through hallway after marble hallway. I rarely showered (mostly because there was hardly any heat where I lived) and showed up to work each morning reeking of booze. On my last day in Philadelphia, I went home with a fellow drunk co-worker, smoked dope, and watched her pass out on the couch. The next day I was back in Vermont, unable to remember how I got there.

I failed my non-resident term. Upon returning to

Bennington after the whole ordeal, a letter to Annette Shapiro, Bennington's non-resident term director, arrived from the museum. The first sentence of the report was, "Michael Klein wreaked havoc upon our mailing list." Which was true. I did pretty much what I felt like and didn't complete most of the work I had been hired for—updating the museum's vast mailing list and filling mail orders for art books.

After Woody fired me, I was in the same mental state Swale must have been in after losing the Lexington Stakes at Keeneland—a state the track photographer captured on grainy film: shock and despair. I was unemployed and disconnected from the horse that had given me the only real joy I had known in the last two years. Steve Crist provided his paper with a sublime coda to his "Renaissance Man" piece that he himself couldn't have dreamed up:

Swale's Groom Dropped
Special to *The New York Times*

BALTIMORE, Md., May 17—Michael Klein, the groom for Swale, the Kentucky Derby winner and favorite for the Preakness Stakes, was discharged from his job this morning by Woody Stephens, the colt's trainer.

According to Stephens and track security officials, Klein caused a disturbance near the colt's stall at about 3 A.M. today and appeared to be intoxicated. He persuaded night watchmen not to call the police, but when Stephens arrived at the stables at 6 A.M. and learned of the incident, he gave Klein air fare back to his home in New York and told him he was dismissed.

Klein could not be located in New York today to discuss

the incident. Telephone calls to his residence on the backstretch at Belmont Park went unanswered. "It's a shame," Stephens said, "because he was a good worker and did right by the horse. But these horses are just too valuable to trust to someone who does his celebrating a few days early."

Stephens then called his stable office at Belmont Park in New York and asked James Reilly, a 22-year-old groom who has been with him for six years, to come to Baltimore immediately and take over as Swale's groom.

Stephens said that Klein, who is 30 years old, would still get his groom's bonus of 1 percent of Swale's Derby winnings, which amounts to $5,347, and might share in his Preakness earnings. Klein had cared for Swale since December 1981, when the colt was a yearling.

When I got back to Belmont, Richard was there to meet me at the front gate, but he had little to say. What could he say? The break-up of Swale and me was the final piece he needed in order to let go once and for all. Woody had cut me loose and now, I suppose, Richard could, too. I was helpless in Richard's eyes, which had lost their innocence and most of their love for me at least a year ago. I had finally lost Richard's respect. At that moment, when I was my most vulnerable and nothing but wreckage, Richard could see me more clearly than he'd ever had. I wasn't the frustrated artist or the passionate lover. I was a drunk who couldn't get sober.

I had been fired the day before the Preakness, so I watched the second jewel on television in a bar. The word around Pimlico was that Swale was overtrained for the Preakness and had come into the race off a blazing workout that just wasn't characteristic of him. On May 19, Swale ran the worst race of his life. Crist reported it was even worse than that:

"Swale's seventh-place finish was the worst by any odds-on favorite in the history of the Preakness and the worst by any favorite since First Landing finished ninth in 1959. The defeat stunned some of his backers, but the depth of his quality had been questioned by many racetrackers who thought he had made a career of beating inferior horses."

I sat in O'Brian's bar and blamed something I couldn't name for Swale's miserable race and for my constitutional incapablility of being honest with myself or straightening up enough at least to hold down a job. Finally, after all these years on the racetrack, I was catching up to myself, and I was heart-broken and weary. And at the end of a long journey. It was as though the years with Swale had all been a dream, as fantastic as the one about the magical horse. I was back in my old life and terrified by the strange and unsettling sensation that I had tampered with fate, that I had interrupted the future and nothing good would ever happen to me again. I was still a groom, but one without horses. For two years, it had been a winning horse that defined me in a business that I never understood completely or even liked that much. In one drunken tirade over guards playing cards in a Baltimore shedrow, all that had changed. Permanently.

Because my share of Swale's stake money would be a long time coming, I had to work. It was usually easy to get a job at Belmont because the turnover in help was so high and every once in a while the feds from INS would come through the barn area like a swarm of locusts and swoop up anyone who didn't have a green card. I got a job all right, but as soon as the foreman realized who I was—a famous drunken groom—I was let go.

I had become unemployable and started living on handouts. I could eat at John the bootlegger's where I could run a tab, and the delicatessen would extend me credit for a month, anyway. In a month things would certainly pan out, or so I figured. It became increasingly clear to me, in this new low of desperation, that I had two choices. I could kill myself or I could stop drinking. But I didn't know the first thing about stopping drinking.

Then something awful happened.

On the morning of June 17, 1984, Swale went to the track for a light workout. It was his first day back in training since capturing the Belmont Stakes nine days before. I had watched the Belmont on television, sure of Swale's victory because, as usual, he was due. Envious and sad, I watched Swale's new groom, Jimmy Reilly, walking the horse onto the track before the race. The sight of groom and horse reiterated the warning I'd gotten from Woody Stephens never to come around the barn area along with the knowledge that I would never see Swale again.

Steve Crist on the Belmont Stakes: "Everyone who ran a horse in the 116th Belmont Stakes yesterday was afraid that Swale would get a slow pace and steal the race, but all they could do was sit back helplessly and watch a perfect crime. The son of Seattle Slew took the lead on the first turn and never relinquished it, coming home an easy four-length winner over Pine Circle yesterday at Belmont Park."

After returning to the barn following that first post-Belmont workout, Swale was bathed as usual. What wasn't usual was that someone other than Jimmy Reilly—a groom for a day—was bathing him. Suddenly, and for no apparent reason, Swale reared up and fell. He thrashed about but couldn't get his bearings. The groom and hotwalker fumbled around, trying to get Swale to his feet, but he wouldn't budge. Everything stopped. All of Woody's barn ran outside and circled the fallen horse. Swale's confirmation suddenly looked false. Those legs never *could* hold all that weight. His tongue and gums went white. He moaned once—something he rarely did in life. And then, quickly and unbelievably, Swale died.

Woody Stephens called Seth Hancock at Claiborne Farm.

"Are you kidding me?" Hancock, astonished, said into the receiver. Seth had been at the Belmont barn just three days earlier and was pleased at how well his colt looked.

"He'll always be my favorite horse," Hancock would say later in the conversation.

Dale Hancock used to tell a story about how, when Swale was a weanling on the farm, you could go into the stall when he was lying down and just sit on his back awhile. Swale would never move and actually seemed to like your being there. He'd pick his head up every now and then to look at you—content like that, stretched out in the heat of the straw. He was always happy for the company—or maybe comforted just in knowing that things stood still. This was the only picture I could hold in my mind, and I held it there all day—Swale's last day on earth.

That summer hour of death was a hard-edged, steamy

one. Everything mute with heat. A day impatient with itself, the kind of day Belmont Park was always ending June on. The Triple Crown races had been run and no horse had won all three. Every contender flops back to mortal again. Which horse was the last to win all three? Seattle Slew? People on the track said my absence was part of the reason Swale threw the Preakness—that a two-year contract between horse and groom had expired, and Swale was dead of a broken heart. A three-hour autopsy turned up nothing to explain Swale's demise. Pathologists and blood specialists walked away with the same news everyone in the barn already knew: that Swale was as sound and healthy a racehorse as anybody had ever seen. With no rational explanation for his death, rumors started circulating Belmont Park like a windstorm—among them, that Swale was sterile, making him useless as a sire. And that I had had something to do with his death.

The day after the autopsy, the New York Racing Association questioned me at length about my movements on the backstretch before Swale died. I had been considered a suspect—actually named as one by Ray Kerrison in a column he wrote for the *New York Post*. After all, I'd been fired by Woody and it wasn't too fantastic to think, especially with some of the minds you get on the racetrack in full tilt boogie, that I had killed Swale for revenge. But more than any bad feelings I may have had for my ex-boss, the track officials were more interested in my drinking life. Their first question to me was if I'd ever been in a blackout.

"I don't know what that is," I told them.

Seventeen

No Horses

Seth Hancock asked the Bourbon Lumber Company to build a box big enough for a horse and then to line it in yellow satin. A racehorse usually gets buried in sections: head, heart, hooves, testicles—the parts the fire is in. I imagine it was Swale's champion status (he won the Eclipse award that year for top three-year-old) that entitled him to full treatment in death. And of course, he was Claiborne's first star, having risen over the farm at a time they needed a star to confirm that it was the right choice to race their own yearlings instead of selling them. The coffin was delivered one bright August morning and everyone who worked at Claiborne Farm took the day off to bury Swale. The champion of so many dreams lies today in the same meadow he got lost in one morning, before he had a name.

I wasn't at that funeral. As public as the death was, due to the media, its aftermath was stunning in its privacy. And so was my broken heart. Stumbling around in amazement and grief is a common sight on the racetrack, so nobody paid any special attention to me. Before Swale's death, I had been seriously contemplating suicide and now I was in shock. I still wanted to die, even more intensely, but the profound loss drained me of the ability to make any kind of decision, rational or irrational. For the first time in my life, drinking was losing its effect. The only way I could see through the first movement of this kind of grief was to have my hand on a racehorse again.

I got a job hotwalking for Mary Cotter, my last official job on the racetrack. I had drunk a lot the night before and was very tired. I fell in the shedrow, still holding onto the horse's shank. Instead of taking off with me the way Aide to Reason had taken off at Latonia, the horse looked down at me in a locked stare. "What are you doing?" the horse seemed to be saying. For the first time since being in the courtroom in Bennington, Vermont, I was in the presence again of something I couldn't touch with my mind. Suddenly, inexplicably, in the silent and frozen stare from a horse came this: *I don't want to drink anymore.* The horse's look went so far inside me that it made me a different person. And this: *You don't have to drink.* Exactly what Richard had been telling me at least once a week for twelve years.

David M., the only person I knew on the track who had gotten sober, took me to Nassau Community Hospital and admitted me to the detox ward. I was put on Librium for five days, attended group therapy sessions, and watched a film called *Chalk Talk,* in which a man named Father Martin talked about the disease of alcoholism. Everything he said went as far inside me as that look the anonymous horse gave me on Mary Cotter's shedrow—the first horse I'd met in all the years on the racetrack whose name I didn't know, which took time back to the beginning of racetrack life, when horses didn't have names yet—the way it was down in Aiken.

A week later I went to Plainview Rehabilitation Center and began the slow process of recovery. The sliver of world going on without me didn't matter anymore. I hadn't given up drinking as much as given in. The date was July 17, 1984. Swale was dead a month.

Eighteen

─────────────

Merton's Fan

Plainview Rehab was once a sanitarium and each room externally connects to the next by a large veranda where, I'd been
told, the staff would roll the patients out in their hospital beds
for doses of sunlight. The hallways there are long and wide
and dark—so dark that it's hard to tell what time of day it is.
The halls seem disconnected from the rest of the building in
that way because the sources of light—from the windows in
the patients' rooms and from the verandas further out—are

too far away for any of it to penetrate the building's central artery. Walking down those halls feels like being on a scavenger hunt through a cave where the prizes at the end are light and time. And, as it happened, the prize of the rest of our lives—if we wanted it.

I got weekend passes after being in the rehab a month and I used to take the bus and train back to Belmont Park to visit Richard, who was still working for Woody. It felt strange, knowing Richard had stayed behind in a barn that had dissolved in my bloodstream along with the Librium the nurse administered in detox to keep me from jumping out of my skin.

Richard and I would meet at the diner across the street from the track—a favorite place of ours. It reminded us of the Famous Diner on Forty-sixth Street and Eighth Avenue where we had gone practically every Sunday morning during the years we lived in Hell's Kitchen. On those visits back to the track, Richard and I would sit in a booth in the silence of amazement over Swale's death and my being sober. It was hard for Richard to face me at the beginning; even in the first months of not drinking, I was already so different—steadier, not looking for an argument. And almost immediately, it seemed, I wasn't nearly as emotionally dependent on him as I had been those many years. It was as though the alcohol had provided the only cause for longing and without it I was actually beginning to enjoy my own company. A sense of wellbeing kept shooting through me like cold water and I became interested in books and music and even clothes again.

And I didn't have the physical desire for alcohol (call it

God or whatever you want—the desire had been lifted from me). Still, it wasn't easy. I shook for three months and couldn't stay awake for more than six or seven hours a day. They told us in rehab that for many recovering drunks, the hardest thing to face in the beginning was what to do with unstructured time. It seemed as if the only thing I could concentrate on was what a book said. I was immersed in Thomas Merton's secular work *No Man Is an Island,* on the one hand, and Thomas à Kempis's sacred *Imitation of Christ,* on the other. I couldn't listen to what people said to me, in the beginning.

Mostly, I was spiritually and psychically exhausted. But after the first few months in rehab when my body and mind started feeling more energetic, I started talking a lot to the other members of my daily therapy group and was eating regularly for the first time in ten years. I also began to understand, the way it must be for a crash victim coming out of a coma, that this was the world I remembered before the accident, and I wanted to live here again.

I was never the kind of alcoholic who went through a period of "laying off the sauce" for a while. I drank to get drunk, to dream, to shift into the blackout I lied and told the track officials I never had. And while it seems so inconceivable that I could actually manage to stop poisoning myself, there was a key in Swale's death that somehow turned the lock in a door that for years had been shut and dead-bolted to me. Swale's was the first death that alcohol couldn't alter the depth of (my mother's death, on the other hand, mixed well with alcohol)— so sobriety was the only choice I had left, if I still wanted to live.

Continuing life has been the leitmotif of abstinence. In a way, it's all you get with sobriety—what some people would term a reprieve is really just holding onto a life you have more interest in. But it all feels like a mystery, somehow.

It's never been easy being sober and, as I said, it didn't come easily—just emphatically. While I don't think Swale would have appeared in my life unless I'd been a active alcoholic (the road out of New York that first trip to River Downs was laid down in inebriation), his death let me get sober. My mother, my lover, and my horse were gone, and something about Swale's vanishing told me it was time to take drastic measures—something clear as day. The blurry effect of a drunk wasn't an appropriate response to a world that had now been emptied of the three great forces of love in my life.

But why credit Mary Cotter's horse, when I could credit God? Because the God I'd felt tremble one time in the voice of a judge dropping charges in Bennington, Vermont, hadn't been heard from for too long, and the horse . . . well, he appeared when I needed him the most, and he wouldn't run off with me. When I first stopped drinking and told some sober friends that a horse got me sober, they all laughed, of course. But then, as quickly as they responded lightheadedly, they went silent. Why *couldn't* it have been a horse leading me out of the fire? In early sobriety, the explainable and unexplainable very often ride the same wave—which makes sobriety different from drunkenness. When you're drunk, only one thing happens.

My years on the track make a great story to tell people I barely know. All of this: the Derby, the drinking, the governor of Kentucky, jail, the lover in and out of my life, so many kinds of dying. And it's twelve years later, and still no one knows what really happened to Swale. Pathologists at the New Bolton Clinic in Pennsylvania spent months looking into his big heart and could find only a small tear there—nothing dreadful enough to have killed him. It will always be a case unsolved, matched in my mind with the conundrum of trying to explain how Swale ever came into my life to begin with.

When I first got to Plainview Rehab, I kept overlaying Swale's story in my mind over the one about the death of Thomas Merton. I'd been reading *The Seven Storey Mountain* and thinking about the electric fan that killed the writer after it toppled over and fell into his Bangkok bathtub. The fan spun madly in my imagination, making it hard to read any of the beautiful sentences Merton had written about his early life, and when it stopped, Swale appeared to me in the most lasting image I will ever have of him, just after he won the Young America Stakes at the Meadowlands:

Black horse.

Snow.

Because it isn't the season for flowers, Swale is wrapped in a blanket of white satin, like a boxer. At one point, before we get back on the van for home, he stops at a paperweight's worth of snow falling in front of the little light over the doorway of one of the concrete barns they have at the Meadowlands, studying its descent.

Or is he?

He nuzzles his big head into my chest because the world is cold again. But by this time, I know he's discovered where the human heart is. We're both so still there in the moment when snow can make you feel warm. The van is waiting, but we're not in a hurry. I'm with the snow and its ambiguous moment with gravity—when the direction of its falling isn't clear. Up or down? The snow can't decide. But in that light, in Swale time, I know all it can do is fall up.